MW00903605

A Brief Biographical History of All T

of the United States

Written By: Steve Kempf

Edited By: Susan Sloate

Introduction

The purpose of this book is to inform twelve year olds, and older or international students who know little, if anything, about the (currently) forty-five presidents, past and present, of the United States. (There are forty-four men who have been U.S. president Grover Cleveland was president from March 4, 1885 to March 4, 1889 and again in March 4, 1893 and March 4, 1897 in nonconsecutive terms.) There is brief biographical information on all forty-five presidents, with interesting notes on their professional accomplishments while in public office.

My hope in writing this work that it shows if an American citizen comes from humble beginnings, he can become President of the United States, if he's willing to work hard enough. This essay also focuses on the two father and son relationships between John Adams and John Quincy Adams. The other father and son relationship George Herbert Walker Bush and George Walker Bush. There is also one case of a direct link from grandfather to grandson, as with William Henry Harrison and Benjamin Harrison. This book also gives birth dates and death dates of thirty-nine presidents, along with the birth dates of the five former presidents who are still living.

The book also looks at the presidential elections such as the 1824, 1876, 1888, and 2000, where electoral votes won the presidential election, not popular votes. This volume also looks at the five major declared wars of the U.S. and their significance. The book also lists several constitutional amendments to the U.S. Constitution and states the significance of each one beginning approximately with the 12th amendment and running through the 27th amendment of the Constitution.

There are three appendices at the end of the book. The first appendix consists of the Declaration of Independence; the second appendix consists of the U.S. Constitution; the third appendix consists of the Bill of Rights. The final section of this work shows two maps: the first map shows the original thirteen colonies. The second map shows the continental United States as it exists today with its forty-eight states.

The 1st President: George Washington

George Washington was the first President of the United States (April 30, 1789-March 4, 1797).

Washington was one of the Founding Fathers of the brand-new United States.

Born: February 22, 1732, Pope Creek Estate in Westmoreland County, Virginia.

Died: December 14, 1799 (aged 67)

Mount Vernon, Virginia.

Education level: The death of his father prevented Washington from acquiring an education at

England's Appleby School, as his older brothers had done. Washington achieved his elementary-level

education through several tutors.

Political Party Affiliation: Unofficially Federalist

Movement of the U.S. Capitol of the United States between 1789 and 1801

Washington took the oath of office for his first term as president in New York City in 1789. During his

second term, Washington took the oath of office in Philadelphia in 1793. (Thomas Jefferson would be

the first sitting president to take the oath of office in the present-day capitol of Washington D.C. in

1801.)

Washington's Domestic Policy

Whiskey Rebellion: 1791 to 1794

The first uprising that Washington had to face in his administration was the Whiskey Rebellion. In

1791 where the Secretary of Treasury Alexander Hamilton came up with the idea of the excise tax to pay the debts that the U.S. government incurred while fighting the American Revolution against the British. Whiskey was used as a form of currency, but the farmers of western Pennsylvania felt that this was too much government interference; they didn't want to pay a tax on their whiskey. In 1794, a group of farmers in western Pennsylvania refused to pay the excise tax.

Washington organized an army of 12,000 men, larger than any army he had led during the American Revolution and went to Pennsylvania. Meanwhile, the men there who had been creating problems dispersed to their respective homes to avoid Washington's army. Washington arrested several their ringleaders and left Pennsylvania.

Background Information on the Significance of Daniel Shay's Rebellions:1786 to 1787

An American Revolutionary war veteran, Daniel Shays, had led a short series of rebellions in Massachusetts between 1786 and 1787, in which Shay's men attempted to seize a federal arsenal of weapons. They were driven off by a state militia commanded by General William Shepard at Springfield, Massachusetts. The significance of the action taken by President George Washington was to show that the new republic backed by the U.S. Constitution would not tolerate insurrections such as the Whiskey Rebellion that occurred between 1791 and 1794 in Pennsylvania nor Shay's Rebellion that had occurred between 1786 and 1787 in Massachusetts under the Articles of Confederation. Whereas under the Articles of Confederation, the federal authorities had been helpless to deal with Shay and so the state authorities in Massachusetts had to deal with Shay themselves. With the creation of the U.S. Constitution, from this time forward, any insurrection or rebellion would be met by force from either the state or federal government or a combination of the two which gave the merchants and politicians, and other wealthy members of American society greater faith in the stability of the American government and society.

The Battle of Fallen Timbers

During his administration, Washington faced a massive battle between the Native Americans and U.S. forces in August 20, 1794, with the Battle of Fallen Timbers, where U.S. forces led by the General Anthony Wayne were able to suppress the Native Americans. The fight involved over two thousand men. When the Native Americans lost this battle, the Ohio Valley was opened to pioneer settlement. Settlers rapidly followed in such large numbers that entirely new states were created, such as Ohio in 1803.

Washington's Foreign Policy

Washington and his three successors, John Adams, Thomas Jefferson, and James Madison would have to deal with the repercussions of the war between Great Britain and France, which would last from 1789 to 1815, the start of the French Revolution and proceeding through the Napoleonic Wars.

Many scholars compared Britain to a shark because of her sea power and France to a tiger because of her land power. Washington also spoke in his farewell speech about entangling alliances with Europe and the constant warfare amongst the European nations. Because the U.S. was in its infancy when it came to military power, Washington supported a neutral policy in dealing with both France and Great Britain. At all cost, he wanted to avoid a war with either world power, while the United States was still so young.

George Washington 1st President of the United States April 30, 1789 to March 4, 1797)
http://www.mountvernon.org/george-washington artwork

The 2nd President: John Adams

John Adams was the second President of the United States (March 4, 1797-March 4, 1801). Adams was also one of the Founding Fathers.

Born: October 30, 1735.

Quincy, Massachusetts

Died: July 4, 1826. (aged 90)

Quincy, Massachusetts

Education: Adams graduated from Harvard in 1755 with a Bachelor of Arts degree. He taught his first couple of years after school and he went back to school and acquired a master's degree. Then he eventually became a lawyer.

Political Party Affiliation: Federalist

President Adams' Domestic Policy

John Adams, in his domestic affairs, was notorious for (with the help of Congress) passing the Alien and Sedition Act of 1798. There were four acts in all, but a few of them are infamous for treading on American civil liberties. The first was the Naturalization Act, which required aliens to live in the United States for fourteen years before becoming citizens, instead of five years as the law had required previously. The Alien Act gave the president the authority to deport any alien that he deemed a threat to American society. Finally, the Sedition Act made it illegal for people to criticize the president and other elected officials. Many newspaper editors who were critical of the president or his cabinet went to jail because of this legislation. These acts only passed because the U.S. was in a quasi-war with France at the time.

President Adams' Foreign Policy

John Adams was able to prevent the U.S. from going to war with France during his Administration because of the strong stance he took against it. Great Britain and France were at war with each other for various reasons. These wars lasted from 1789 to 1815.

John Adams was known as the Father of the U.S. Navy, because of his work to build up a strong federal navy instead of relying on privateers (critics would say pirates) to hurt either the British or French navies.

However, it was not easy dealing with either France or Great Britain, diplomatically. In France, the government was notorious for its corruption. One French government official told the American diplomatic delegation with whom he was to discuss a possible treaty that he would not talk to them unless they paid him a bribe, that may have been as high as $250,000. The American delegation refused angrily and left. It became known as the 'X-Y-Z Affair.'

John Adams 2nd President of the United States (March 4, 1797 to March 4, 1801)
https://www.gettyimages.ch/detail/nachrichtenfoto/portrait-of-john-adams-american-

politician-2nd-nachrichtenfoto/930103998#portrait-of-john-adams-american-politician-2nd-president-

of-the-picture-id930103998

The 3rd President: Thomas Jefferson

Thomas Jefferson was the third President of the United States (March 4, 1801-March 4, 1809).

Jefferson was also one of the Founding Fathers. Jefferson and James Madison were the founders of the

Democratic-Republican party, which controlled both the presidency and Congress, until James Monroe

left office in 1829.

Born: April 13, 1743

Shadwell, Va.

Died: July 4, 1826 (aged 83)

Monticello, Va.

Education: Jefferson was a tremendous student, starting an English class at the age of five and then a

Latin class at the age of nine. Jefferson started William & Mary College in 1760 and finished in 1762,

with a bachelor's degree. Jefferson was known to study fifteen hours a day. He studied law under

George Wythe, and eventually became a lawyer, before becoming a politician.

Political Party Affiliation: Democratic-Republican

The Presidential Election of 1800

12th Constitutional Amendment (1804): This amendment was passed in response to the 1800

Presidential Election, in which both the president and the vice-president, Thomas Jefferson and Aaron

Burr, received the exact same number of electoral votes: 73 each. The Federalist, incumbent President

John Adams received 64 electoral votes, and his vice-presidential running mate, Charles Pinckney of South Carolina, received 63 electoral votes. To prevent this from happening again, if there is ever a dispute over the electoral votes, the House of Representatives will decide the presidential election and the Senate will decide the electoral votes for the vice-president. Congress also added the extra step that the electors can vote only ONE vote per president and ONE vote per vice-president. This is what led to trouble before; some electors used their two votes to vote EITHER for the president or for the vice-president. With the passage of the 12th Amendment, which took effect in 1804, this amendment required that each voter put his name and the name of the candidate for who he was voting, whether president or vice-president. Before the passage of the 12th Amendment, the electoral college would add up all the votes for the president and whoever had the most electoral votes became president; whoever came in second became vice-president. This led to many problems, which the 12th Amendment helped to correct.

1804 Presidential Election

In the 1804 presidential election, the incumbent Democrat-Republican Thomas Jefferson crushed Charles Pinckney: Jefferson got 162 electoral votes to Pinckney's 12. George Clinton became Thomas Jefferson's vice-president. George Clinton served not only Jefferson but his successor James Madison as well.

Jefferson's Domestic Policy

In 1803, Napoleon offered to sell to the U.S., for $15-million, the land that became known as The Louisiana Purchase. The Louisiana Purchase effectively doubled the size of the United States but cost only about three cents an acre. Out of this territory would later come fifteen new states and territories.

The Louisiana Purchase comprised seven future whole states: Louisiana, Iowa, Arkansas, Missouri, Nebraska, North Dakota, and South Dakota. It also included what became the territories of Mississippi, Alabama, Montana, Colorado, Wyoming, Oklahoma, and Minnesota. President Jefferson also authorized the exploration of the West when he persuaded explorers William Clark and Meriwether Lewis to organize an expedition to explore the new territory. This expedition would last from 1804 to 1806. The Lewis and Clark expedition (also known as the Corps of Discoverers) traveled from St. Louis, Missouri approximately 8,000 miles, going down the Ohio River, up the Missouri River and across the Continental Divide, and then to the Pacific Ocean. Lewis was a jack-of-all-trades, acting as an historian, botanist, zoologist, meteorologist, ethnographic, and geographer of the expedition. Tragically, Lewis would commit suicide on October 11, 1809.

Jefferson's Foreign Policy

Jefferson created the Embargo Act in 1807 to retaliate against Britain, because the British were seizing American ships and kidnapping (impressing) American sailors whom they forced to work on their own naval ships, claiming that the U.S was illegally trading with France, their sworn enemy. President Jefferson hoped his embargo would hurt the British economy, because the U.S. would no longer trade with them. He hoped in the long term, this would help American farmers.

Unfortunately, neither of these things happened. British consumers and merchants put up with the U.S. embargo. And American farmers, especially in New England, were ready to rebel against the U.S. government, because their unsold grain, which usually went to Britain, was slowly rotting away.

Thomas Jefferson 3rd President of the United States(March 4, 1801 to March 4, 1809) http.www.history.com./topics/-uspresidents-thomasjefferson/pictures

The 4th President: James Madison

James Madison was the 4th president (March 4, 1809-March 4, 1817). Madison was also one of the Founding Fathers.

Born: March 16, 1751

Port Conway, Va.

Died: June 28, 1836 (aged 85)

Montpelier, Va.

Education: Princeton University (1769-1771) (bachelor's degree).

Political Party Affiliation: Democratic-Republican

War of 1812 and the Causes of the War of 1812

During Madison's presidency, the U.S. declared war against Great Britain (on June 18, 1812), because of such issues as impressment. The British Navy would stop American vessels and seize American sailors, claiming they were former British sailors who had left the British Navy and joined the American Navy because the American Navy paid higher wages. Both the French and British Navies were seizing American vessels at this time, but the American public had greater animosity toward the British than the French because of the American Revolution, which had not happened so long before only about thirty years). The French had been America's allies during the American Revolution.

A secondary consideration was that the British secretly hoped to win back the American states in this war, which eventually became known as the 'second war of independence'. The states had been on their own since 1783, but Britain thought that if they won, they could take back and re-tame the new American states. They were quite prepared to fight, if they could regain these valuable lands again.

Canada was also considered a valuable prize, which was there for the taking, by war hawks such as Henry Clay. The British had supported rebellious Native American tribes along the Great Lakes region, and these tribes had made deadly raids against Americans in the area. America began the war with great enthusiasm, but after several failed invasions of Canada, Americans were depressed about their progress in the war.

The Battle of Lake Erie

The Battle of Lake Erie occurred in 1813, on Lake Erie. The naval commander of the American fleet was Oliver Hazard Perry. Perry put into Presque Isle (modern-day Erie, Pennsylvania), where he commissioned several carpenters to build him a naval fleet. The British, under their commander, Robert Heriot Barclay, had started building a naval fleet of their own as well. (The Americans would eventually have nine ships while the British had six ships). The two forces were ready for combat on September 10, 1813, and the initial meeting of the naval forces favored the British, with their longer range guns; however, the Americans were eventually able to get closer to the British. By constantly raking the British ships with cannon fire, the Americans finally defeated the British after the day-long battle and captured their entire fleet. This battle is important, because when the British lost this battle, they could no longer use the Great Lakes region as a base of operations. The British also had to abandon Detroit and retreat on foot back toward Canada. At the end of the battle, the American naval commander sent a famous message to his commanding officer (and later president) William Henry Harrison: "We have met the enemy; they are ours." Victory here also set up another victory for American forces, when the American forces met and defeated the British and Native American forces at the Battle of the Thames in Canada on October 5, 1813.

The Battle of Blandesburg

16

The Battle of Blandesburg occurred on August 24, 1814, between British and American forces. When the American forces lost this battle, the British pushed into the Washington D.C. area and burned the new American capitol, including the White House, and several buildings in the surrounding area. President Madison and his wife, family, and staff had to flee; otherwise they would have been captured by British forces.

The Battle of Plattsburgh

Americans had another significant victory in the naval battle at Plattsburgh, New York on September 11, 1814, where American naval forces under the leadership of Thomas Macdonough were able to repulse the attack and destroy the British naval fleet; the British had to retreat on foot back to Canada. Had the British won this battle, it could have led to New York's being split from the rest of the U.S.

Attack on Fort McHenry

Another important battle on September 13-14, 1814 was the British naval ships bombarding of Fort McHenry. If Fort McHenry fell to the British, this would leave Baltimore open to invasion by British forces and would give the British a better opportunity to establish a base of operations in Maryland and harass the capitol city of Washington D.C. This was also a chance for the British to punish Baltimore, which was a hotbed of anti-British sentiment at the time. When the fort withstood the bombardment for over twenty-four hours, the British had to abandon their military enterprise. A young lawyer named Francis Scott Key was aboard a British ship in the harbor during this battle, and watching the bombs bursting over a giant American flag flying at the fort, he was inspired to write a poem which he called "The Star-Spangled Banner". This poem, set to music, would later become America's national anthem.

The Battle of New Orleans

The most significant battle that the U.S. won was the Battle of New Orleans on January 8, 1815. The Americans, inexperienced volunteers who were vastly outnumbered by the experienced British force, were led by General Andrew Jackson. Jackson's forces won, but ironically, the war had actually been over for two weeks when the battle began, because the Treaty of Ghent ending hostilities between the two countries had been signed on December 24, 1814. The news had not yet reached U.S. and British military forces in time to stop the battle.

After the War of 1812, Madison set up pension plans for widows and orphans for five years; he also set up the Tariff Act of 1816 to protect American industries from foreign competition. He signed legislation that created a new Bank of the United States for twenty years. After the War of 1812, peace followed for some years, which began what historians have labeled "The Era of Prosperity". Historians generally believe James Madison had a very successful presidency, and consistently list him among the top ten best presidents of the U.S.

James Madison 4th President of the United States (March 4, 1809 to March 4, 1817)

https://www.britannica.com/biography/James-Madison

The 5th President: James Monroe

James Monroe was the 5th President of the United States (March 4, 1817-March 4, 1825). He is one of the Founding Fathers.

Born: April 28, 1758

Monroe Hall, Va.

Died: July 4, 1831 (aged 73)

New York City, New York

Education: He attended Campbell Academy in 1769, where he met John Marshall (future Supreme Court Justice). He also entered William & Mary in 1774 and earned a bachelor's degree. After the American Revolution, he studied law under Thomas Jefferson.

Political Party Affiliation: Democratic-Republican

James Monroe presided over the "Era of Good Feelings", when the Federalists and Anti-Federalists had come to terms with each other. The Federalist party was fading away and would eventually become the Whig party.

A painting of Monroe was created by Samuel Morse, who had a career as a painter before he invented the telegraph in 1844. In 1821, James Monroe established Liberia as a colony for former slaves to go back to Africa. In fact, Monrovia is the only capital of another country named after a U.S. president in the entire world!

The Compromise of 1820

The Compromise of 1820 was the result of a legislative problem. At that time, Missouri was one of the new states coming out of the land gained in the Louisiana Purchase (1803), which threatened to upset the balance of free states and slave states in the Union. Eventually, Congress worked out a compromise, which provided for Missouri and everything north of the 36' 30 parallel to be a free (non-slave) state, and everything below it to permit slavery. Missouri, or part of it, would come into the Union as a slave state; Maine would come in as a free state. In 1820, after this compromise, there would be twenty-four United States: twelve free states and twelve slave states. This important compromise occurred during President Monroe's Administration.

The Monroe Doctrine of 1823

Though his Secretary of State John Quincy Adams was the real author of the Monroe Doctrine in December 2, 1823, the Monroe Doctrine was an important part of Monroe's presidency, and did capture how many Americans felt about the older, bigger European powers and their desire to re-establish their military and political power over their former colonies. Case in point was with the revolt of Mexico in 1810: all of Spain's colonies in Latin America except Puerto Rico and Cuba were lost to them by 1826. The U.S. was also concerned about the Spanish in Florida and about Russia in California. President Monroe's doctrine essentially told the Europeans to keep their hands off the New World and their former colonies.

Ironically, Great Britain, with its great Navy, made sure that Spain, Russia, and France would not take over any new territories because Britain wanted to keep its trade with Latin America, which it had established once the Spanish were kicked out of their former colonies.

James Monroe 5th President of the United States
(March 4, 1817 to March 4, 1825)
www.google.com-jamesmadison

The 6th President: John Quincy Adams

John Quincy Adams was the 6th President of the United States (March 4, 1825-March 4, 1829). He was the first president who was also the son of a president (John Adams).

Born: July 11, 1767

Braintree (Quincy), Massachusetts

Died: February 23, 1848 (aged 80)

Washington, D.C.

Education: Adams' parents taught him mathematics, languages, and the classics at home. In 1778, John Quincy Adams accompanied his father to Europe, where he studied at the Passy Academy outside Paris, and learned dancing, fencing, music, and art. John Quincy Adams graduated from Harvard in 1785, with a bachelor's degree and a master's degree. After college, Adams studied law and passed the bar exam in 1790.

Political Party Affiliation: Democratic-Republican (1808-1830)

The Presidential Election of 1824

The Presidential election of 1824 was one of the most hotly-contested political elections in presidential history. There were five candidates: John C. Calhoun, William Crawford, Henry Clay, Andrew Jackson, and John Quincy Adams. For the first time in presidential history, nobody won a clear majority of electoral votes. Henry Clay, who was the Speaker of the House of Representatives and the highest-ranking Congressman at the time, threw his support behind John Quincy Adams; Adams ended up winning the presidential election.

Jackson and his supporters screamed about a "Corrupt Bargain"; this would haunt Adams throughout his presidency, as Jackson's political supporters, both in the U.S. Congress and elsewhere, blocked Adam's domestic legislation at every turn. Jackson had won a plurality of 99 electoral votes and 153,544 popular votes while John Quincy Adams had 84 electoral votes and 108,740 popular votes. However, since Jackson did not have a majority electoral vote, the House of Representatives had to decide the presidential election. This is the first time and only time that the House of Representatives invoked the Twelfth Amendment of the Constitution, where the House would decide the presidential election. When Henry Clay gave his 37 electoral votes to Adams, this increased Adams' total to 121 electoral votes; thus the majority, and therefore the election, belonged to Adams. Once Adams became president he made Henry Clay his Secretary of State, which at the time was often a stepping stone to becoming the next President of the United States. The whole affair appeared to be one of a quid pro quo "something for something"; this is why Jackson and his supporters were screaming about "the corrupt bargain."

Education and Background Information on President John Quincy Adams and his Aloofness

President John Quincy Adams was a brilliant Harvard-educated man (like his father) who was also ambassador to Russia in his younger years. He was also posted to Prussia, the Netherlands and Great Britain. Besides Russian, he could also speak French, and several other languages (seven altogether). Unfortunately, he was not socially adept, and often came off as cold and standoffish. However, politics was entering a new phase, where voters did not show as much unquestioned deference to their political leaders but expected them to be able to interact with them. Adams' aloof personality was a distinct liability.

When Andrew Jackson later ran for the U.S. presidency in 1824, he was a popular figure because he was the hero of the Battle of New Orleans (1815).

Adams' Accomplishment During His Presidency:

Adams did not have many accomplishments in office, because Jackson and his supporters were determined to thwart them at every turn. However, two of his biggest accomplishments were signing the legislation that would eventually lead to the creation of the United States Naval Observatory (USNO) and his support for the creation of the Smithsonian Institute, though this did not officially occur until 1846.

However, Adams did have an energetic and impressive post-presidency. He was the only ex-president to run for—and win—a seat in the House of Representatives. He also argued before the Supreme Court for the African slaves on the slave ship *Amistad*.

In 1846 he suffered a stroke while on the floor of the House of Representatives. Two years later, he died.

John Quincy Adams 6th President of the United States
(March 4, 1825 to March 4, 1829)
http://cdn.loc.gov/service/pnp/cph/3a50000/3a53000/3a53200/3a53280v.jpg

The 7th President of the United States: Andrew Jackson

Andrew Jackson was the 7th President of the United States (March 4, 1829-March 4, 1837).

Born: March 11, 1767

Birthplace: Waxhaws settlement (Carolinas)

Died: June 8, 1845 (aged 78)

The Hermitage Nashville, Tennessee.

Education: Private tutors educated Andrew Jackson at an early age. At the age of 15, Jackson went to school, before becoming a lawyer in 1787. (He has no college education).

Political Party Affiliation: Democratic Party

The Presidential Election of 1828

The election of 1828 featured a rematch between the incumbent president, John Quincy Adams, and the Democratic challenger, Andrew Jackson. Jackson and Adams were the only candidates in the 1828 presidential election, unlike the 1824 presidential election, where there had been five candidates.

This time Jackson easily defeated Adams in the electoral college: 178 to 83, and in the popular vote: 647,286 to 508,064.

John C. Calhoun was Jackson's first vice-president, with whom Jackson did not particularly get along. He said once that he had only two regrets: "that I have not shot Henry Clay or hanged John C. Calhoun."

The Presidential Election of 1832

Four candidates ran in the 1832 election. Andrew Jackson, the Democratic incumbent, easily defeated Henry Clay, with 219 electoral votes to Clay's 49 electoral votes. Jackson bested Clay in popular votes, with Jackson winning 607,582 to Clay's 530,189. The two other candidates, John Floyd (independent) had 11 electoral votes, all from South Carolina. His popular-vote total is unknown. The anti-Masonic politician William Wirt (a third-party candidate running in a third party for the first time in American history) won 7 electoral votes and 101,501 popular votes.

Martin van Buren was Jackson's second vice-president and ran successfully for the presidency in 1836. (This feat of a vice-president succeeding a president would not be repeated until George Herbert Walker Bush became president in 1989.)

The Attempted Assassination of President Andrew Jackson

On January 30, 1835, Richard Lawrence tried to assassinate him with two different pistols; both misfired! When the second pistol misfired, Jackson attacked the man with his cane and beat him until authorities separated them. Later, the police tried both pistols and they both functioned perfectly! Scholars estimate the chances of this happening at 125,000 to 1.

Andrew Jackson has the dubious distinction of being the first president to face attempted assassination.

The Nullification Crisis

In 1828 and again in 1832, a tariff rate was passed that the South thought was excessive, because it seemed to favor the rapidly industrializing North. Some Southern states, especially South Carolina, found it offensive because it raised the tariff rate to an exorbitant amount. South Carolina claimed that they nullify the tariff legislation, claiming that the South Carolina government had the right to do that to any federal legislation that they found offensive.

Both Congress and the President reacted strongly, with Congress passing the Force Bill, authorizing the President to take whatever military actions he deemed necessary to enforce this legislation.

President Jackson threatened to have tens of thousands of military personnel in South Carolina within forty days if South Carolina did not comply with the tariff law. Fortunately, cooler heads worked behind the scenes on a bill that would slowly reduce the amount of tariff that the American South would pay, so they avoided armed conflict at that point. Henry Clay worked out the Tariff Bill of 1833, which reduced the tariff rate in ten years to the amount that the tariff had been in 1816.

The Indian Removal Act

Jackson signed the Indian Removal Act in 1830, to force Native Americans in the southeastern states to move west of the Mississippi. Georgia began deporting the Cherokee nation from within their borders because Georgian residents wanted the Cherokee land. The Cherokee nation was a civilized Native American tribe that had adopted many of the White man's ways, including slavery.

The Cherokees took their case all the way to the U.S. Supreme Court. The Court decided in their favor and Chief Justice John Marshall wrote that the state of Georgia had no right to evict the Cherokees from their ancestral home. President Jackson is reported to have replied, "John Marshall has made his decision; now let him enforce it." When the president took no action to protect the Cherokee, Georgia's militia forced the Cherokee Indians all the way west to what is now the state of Oklahoma. This whole event is called "The Trail of Tears"; as many as 15,000 Cherokees were forced to walk to Oklahoma and as many as 25 percent died of exposure and disease.

Other Highlights: Andrew Jackson

Jackson is credited with creating the modern Democratic party when he was elected in 1828. He chose the donkey for its symbol. He is also credited with giving the common man the right to vote and to expand it to 'universal suffrage': even if you owned no property and paid no taxes, if you were white and male, you could vote. Jackson also opened the British West Indies to American trade, through a treaty with Great Britain. Jackson also opened trade to Asian nations as well; by one estimate, he increased American exports by 70 percent and American imports by 250 percent.

Andrew Jackson 7th President of the United States
(March 4, 1829 to March 4, 1837)
http://cdn.loc.gov/service/pnp/pga/11900/11931v.jpg

The 8th President: Martin Van Buren

Martin Van Buren was the 8th President of the United States (March 4, 1837-March 4, 1841).

Born: December 5, 1782

Kinderhook, NY

Died: July 24, 1862 (aged 79)

Kinderhook, NY

Education: Van Buren studied English and Latin at the local school until he was fourteen. Then he studied under a lawyer and eventually became a New York lawyer in 1803. (He has no college education.)   .

Political Party Affiliation: Democratic Party

By most accounts, President Martin van Buren inherited a recession from his predecessor Andrew Jackson, because of the former president's war with the Bank of the United States. Banks in New York City started to fail when they refused to give either gold or silver back for paper money. England also went through its own Depression, where there was less money for the English to pay for cotton, which affected American farmers in the South. Van Buren also came out against annexing the state of Texas, because Texas was a slave state.

In 1838-1839, a local war erupted between Maine and Canada lumbermen over a dispute of land between Maine and New Brunswick, Canada, because the boundaries were ambiguous. This dispute went back to the American Revolution in 1783, and the signing of the peace treaty between Britain and America. This dispute became known as the Aroostook War, and was resolved by van Buren and Great

Britain.

The international incident involving the mutiny on the slave ship *Amistad* occurred during his presidency (July 2, 1839-November 26, 1841). The defense lawyer for the former slaves in this legal case was former U.S. president John Quincy Adams. The *Amistad* legal case was appealed to the U.S. Supreme Court and took two and a half years to resolve, before the fifty-three former slaves involved in the mutiny were granted their freedom.

Martin Van Buren 8th President of the United States (March 4, 1837, to March 4, 1841)
https://www.history.com/topics/us-presidents/martin-van-buren/pictures/martin-van-buren/painted-

portrait-of-martin-van-buren

The 9th President: William Henry Harrison

Born: February 9, 1773

Berkeley Plantation, Va.

Died: April 4, 1841 (aged 68)

The White House, Washington, D.C.

Education: W.H. Harrison was privately tutored at home, then attended Hampton-Sydney College in Virginia. His father wanted him to become a doctor, so Harrison went to Philadelphia to study at Benjamin Rush; however, his father died in 1791 and the estate went to his older brothers. With no money to continue his studies, Harrison pursued a military career instead. (He has no college education).

Political Party Affiliation: Whig

William Henry Harrison was the 9th President of the United States (1841). He was inaugurated on March 4, 1841, and gave the longest inaugural speech in presidential history, which lasted approximately two hours. Sadly, President Harrison refused to wear a coat while giving his speech; it was cold outside, and he caught a cold that turned into pneumonia. He died on April 4, 1841 in the Oval Office, the first president to die in office. President Harrison, with one month in office, had the shortest presidential administration in U.S. history.

31

William Henry Harrison 9ᵗʰ President of the United States (March 4, 1841
to April 4, 1841)
https://en.wikipedia.org/wiki/William_Henry_Harrison#/media/File:Bass_Otis_(American,_1784-1861)_-_Portrait_of_William_Henry_Harrison.jpg

The 10th President: John Tyler

John Tyler was the 10th President of the United States (April 4, 1841-March 4, 1845).

Born: March 29, 1790

Charles City County, Va.

Died: January 18, 1862 (aged 71)

Richmond, Va.

Education: At the age of twelve, Tyler entered preparatory school for William & Mary College. Three years later, he entered the formal college of William and Mary and graduated in 1807 with a bachelor's degree. He then studied law and passed the bar exam and became a lawyer in 1809 at the age of nineteen.

Political Party Affiliation: Whig

When W.H. Harrison died on April 4, 1841, this created the first succession crisis of the presidency because W.H. Harrison was the first president to die in office. His Vice-President, John Tyler, declared that he was the new president, with all the acting powers of the president. (This view would not be officially recognized until the passage of the 25th Constitutional amendment in 1967). Tyler is one of only two presidents (the other being Chester Arthur) not to have a vice-president, because he refused to appoint one while he was president. Tyler was also the first president to be called the "accidental president" a label that would be applied to other presidents, including Gerald Ford.

President Tyler was a member of the Whig party, but when two members of his party, Henry Clay and Daniel Webster, wanted to create a new U.S. bank, Tyler refused because he believed that the U.S. bank would have too much financial power. The Whig party was so incensed over this and other actions that President Tyler took while in office that Tyler was expelled from the Whig party while he was President!

Before he left office, Tyler handled another thorny political issue. Texas had won its independence from Mexico and declared itself a Republic, but no president or other politician wanted to touch this issue because Texas permitted slavery, which could potentially divide the North and the South, who each jockeyed for power through the number of states which were slave states and free states.

President Tyler had the U.S. Congress adopt a joint resolution that brought Texas into the Union on March 3, 1845, the day before he left office on March 4, 1845.

John Tyler 10th President of the United States (April 4, 1841, to March 4, 1845)

http://cdn.loc.gov/service/pnp/cph/3a50000/3a53000/3a53200/3a53283r.jpg

The 11th President: James Polk

James Knox Polk was the 11th President of the United States (March 4, 1845-March 4, 1849).

Born: November 2, 1795

Mecklenburg County North Carolina

Died: June 15, 1849 (aged 53)

Nashville, Tennessee

Education: Polk was educated by his mother and private tutors. He entered the University of North

Carolina in 1816, graduated in 1818 (bachelor's degree), studied law under Felix Grundy and passed

the bar in 1820.

Political Party: Democratic Party

President Polk's Foreign and Domestic Policy

James Knox Polk came into office with clear objectives in mind. He approved the joint resolution

that joined Texas to the Union and eventually engaged U.S. forces in a war with Mexico (1846-1848).

This war would become popular with the American public because of the belief at the time in Manifest

Destiny, the belief that it was America's destiny to rule from sea to shining sea. (the Atlantic to the

Pacific coasts.)

The following timeline outlines the important events of the Mexican-American War 1846-1848.

January 1846—President Polk ordered General Zachary Taylor to send troops to the Rio Grande.

April 25, 1846—Mexican troops fired on U.S. troops and killed fourteen U.S. soldiers.

May 11, 1846—President Polk asked for a declaration of war with Mexico during a joint session of

Congress.

May 13, 1846—Congress approved going to war with Mexico.

Summer 1846—The U.S. Navy occupied Monterrey, California.

February 22 to February 23, 1847—At the Battle of Buena Vista, General Zachary Taylor defeated a Mexican army. His victory made General Taylor a national hero; this would lead to Taylor's eventually becoming president in 1849.

March 1847—The fortress of Vera Cruz was considered impregnable, but it fell to American forces within three weeks.

 Summer 1847—A second army under the command of General Winfield Scott began moving toward Mexico City.

September 13-14—This American army defeated the Mexicans at the Battle of Chapultepec.

September 12-September 15—American forces defeated the Mexicans at Mexico City and occupied Mexico City.

February 2, 1848—With Mexico City commanded by the American military, the Mexican-American War came to an end with the Treaty of Guadalupe Hidalgo.

This war would result in the United States acquiring territory which became the states of Utah, Nevada, and California. The U.S. also acquired partial territories in New Mexico, Arizona, Colorado and Wyoming.

President Polk resolved the sectional dispute with the British over the territory of Oregon (which today is Oregon and Washington state), where it seemed both countries were ready to go to war. To administer these new territories, the Department of the Interior was created.

Polk did not run for re-election. He felt he had done what he came to Washington to do. Within a couple of months of leaving the White House to return home to Tennessee, he died.

James K. Polk 11th President of the United States (March 4, 1845 to
March 4, 1849)
https://www.google.com/search?=Portrait+of+James+K.+Polk

The 12th President: Zachary Taylor

Zachary Taylor was the 12th President of the United States (March 4, 1849-July 9, 1850).

Born: November 24, 1784

Barboursville, Va.

Died: July 9, 1850 (aged 65)

Washington D.C.

Education: He was educated by a teacher who coached him more than taught him. President Taylor was known to have terrible handwriting (No college education).

Political Party Affiliation: Whig

Zachary Taylor was the Whig president who had been a war hero, as a general in the Mexican-American War (1846-1848). Unhappily, he was only president for a little over sixteen months.

This was a time of great sectional hostility between the North and the South over slavery. Though President Taylor was a slave owner, he believed in the unity of the American states over the South's right to secede from the Union to keep the institution of slavery. However, before President Taylor could take any action on this issue, he became ill, eating cherries and drinking milk on the

Fourth of July 1850. He died five days later, on July 9, 1850.

Zachary Taylor 12th President of the United States (March 4, 1849 to July
9, 1850)
https://www.google.com/search?=Portrait of Zachary Taylor

The 13th President of the United States: Millard Fillmore

Millard Fillmore was the 13th President of the United States (July 9, 1850-March 4, 1853).

Born: January 7, 1800

Cayuga County, N.Y.

Died: March 8, 1874 (aged 74)

Buffalo, N.Y.

Education: six months of grade school; read law in 1822 became a lawyer then. (No college education).

Political Party Affiliation: Whig

With the death of Zachary Taylor on July 9, 1850, Millard Fillmore, who was Taylor's vice-president, became the president of the United States through the succession laws of the U.S. Constitution. President Fillmore took an active interest in keeping the Union together, so he would actively work with such Democratic leaders as Stephen Douglas on what would be called the Compromise of 1850.

The Compromise of 1850

The Compromise of 1850 was comprised of several legislative acts that came out of the Mexican-American War (1846-1848). California was coming into the Union as a free state; this would once more upset the balance of states between slave states and free states; at this point, there would be more free states than slave states. California was admitted to the Union as a free state, and there was a border dispute that had to be worked out between Texas and New Mexico. The power of the Fugitive Slave

Act of 1793 was greatly increased with a new Fugitive Slave Law in 1850, with deputies being responsible for bringing back fugitive slaves in the North. If law enforcement officials refused to do this, they could be charged $1,000 dollars (in 1850 dollars!) and if the slave escaped under their watch, the law enforcement official in charge was responsible for paying the former master of the slave the full amount of what the slave was worth. Utah was also brought in as a territory, which could later decide whether if it wanted to be slave or a free state. As the final law in the Compromise, the District of Columbia became a free territory.

Millard Fillmore 13th President of the United States (July 9, 1850, to
March 4, 1853)
http://cdn.loc.gov/service/pnp/cwpbh/00600/00699v.jpg

The 14th President of the United States: Franklin Pierce

Franklin Pierce was the 14th President of the United States (March 4, 1853-March 4, 1857).

Born: November 23, 1804

Hillsboro New Hampshire Died:

October 8, 1869 (aged 64)

Concord, NH

Education: Bowdoin College: (bachelor's degree) Northampton Law School;

Political Party: Northern Democrat

The Kansas-Nebraska Act of 1854

Franklin Pierce became president as the battle over territory and slavery heated up, and it was marked by tragedy, when the President-elect and his wife Jane were on a train that derailed, a few months before the inauguration. The accident killed their eleven-year-old son Bennie, which devastated Jane, who had lost two other sons to early deaths.

While Pierce had been a U.S. Congressman for years, but he was not really prepared for the pressures of the presidency. Very soon, the Kansas-Nebraska Act was introduced. The bill stirred up a political hornets' nest, by proposing that Kansas and Nebraska settle for themselves the question of whether they wanted slavery or not in their states, which Pierce thought had been settled in the

Compromise of 1850, but which pro-slavery people were determined to open again. This idea was

known as popular sovereignty. The strongest proponent of popular sovereignty was Senator Stephen

Douglas of Illinois. Pierce gave in to the pro-slavery people and signed the bill into law, but it led to

anarchy and chaos as citizens took the law into their own hands.

Soon came the Pottawatomie Massacre in Kansas, on May 24-May 25, 1856, in which several

slave owners were murdered in front of their families, by John Brown and his cohorts. John Brown said

his attack was retaliating for the pro-slavery forces that had sacked the town of Lawrence, Kansas on

May 21, 1856, because of the anti-slavery forces that lived there.

Pierce could not hold the confidence of his own party, and for the first time, when the

Democrats held a convention to choose their presidential nominee, the sitting president did not receive

their nomination.

Pierce left Washington in 1857, went home to New Hampshire and returned to his law practice.

Franklin Pierce 14th President of the United States
(March 4, 1853 to March 4, 1857)
http://cdn.loc.gov/service/pnp/cph/3a50000/3a53000/3a53200/3a53287r.jpg

The 15th President: James Buchanan

James Buchanan was the 15th President of the United States (March 4, 1857-March 4, 1861).

Born: April 23, 1791

Cove Gap Pennsylvania

Died: June 1, 1868 (aged 77)

Lancaster, Pennsylvania

Education: Dickinson College: Bachelor's degree

Political party: Democratic

James Buchanan was the only president who never married. He was a lifelong bachelor, and there were rumors that he was homosexual, because until he was elected president, he had lived with another man, Rufus King, for approximately ten years in a Washington D.C. boarding house, though he was never proven to be a homosexual. His niece, Harriet Lane, acted as his hostess and greeted guests to the Oval Office. In fact, Harriet Lane is where the term First Lady comes from because Harriet Lane was Buchanan's niece and not his wife so First Lady was a term used to describe her status at the White House.

Unfortunately for President Buchanan, the U.S. was moving closer and closer to a civil war, and he was an indecisive leader. He had no personal interest in slavery but was willing to accede to the pro-slavery forces if it would keep peace in the Union. He also felt that the Constitution did not give the government the power to prevent states from seceding from the Union.

In 1857, the Dred Scott decision landmark legal case made things worse. Chief Justice Roger B. Taney wrote the majority opinion that slaves had no legal or civil rights in the United States and that the U.S. Congress had no legal authority to deal with slavery or to even deal with the constitutional issue of territories which would become future American states.

This caused a great furor. Many white Southerners were happy with the decision, while many white Northerners were angry. Some Northerners called for opposition to the Supreme Court's decision, with such prominent Northern politicians as William Seward claiming that "there is a higher law than the Constitution, which regulates our authority over the domain, and devotes it to the same noble purpose" and implied that Americans should follow their consciences, even if that meant breaking the law.

The Lecompton Constitution in Kansas in 1857 created more tension, as it was drafted by an illegal pro-slavery legislature and argued for a pro-slavery point of view for Kansas. President Buchanan showed poor judgment in pushing the law, as only a minority of Kansas voters had approved in the first place. The U.S. Congress voted in 1858 to accept Kansas into the Union as a slave state, though most Kansas voters wanted the state to be a free state.

James Buchanan 15th President of the United States (March 4, 1857 to March 4,

1861)www.google.com

The 16th President: Abraham Lincoln

Abraham Lincoln was the 16th President of the United States (March 4, 1861-April 15, 1865).

Born: February 12, 1809

Sinking Spring Farm, near Hodgenville, Kentucky.

Died: April 15, 1865 (aged 56)

Petersen House, Washington D.C.

Education: (No college education) Lawyer by training

Political Party Affiliation: Republican

Abraham Lincoln became President of the United States in one of the most troubling periods in our history. The Southern Confederacy, a group of slave-holding states, had seceded from the United States, because of their fear that Lincoln as President would outlaw slavery and destroy their economy. They had already formed a separate government and were hoping for recognition from Great Britain and France.

Lincoln knew that he had to act but did not want to trigger a war. His great concern was that a country split in half was not strong enough to survive, and unlike others, for whom slavery was the primary issue, Lincoln believed strongly that the Union had to remain unified, if the United States was to remain a viable country at all.

When South Carolina seized Fort Sumter, in the Charleston Harbor, Lincoln decided to send arms and other supplies—but not an army—to Fort Sumter. South Carolina saw this as an insult to them and fired on the fort on April 12, 1861, and this hostile act began the Civil War.

Lincoln said the seven Southern states that comprised the Confederacy were in secession and that the other states should sent volunteers to Washington to make up new armies to fight the South. Regrettably, with this call from Lincoln, four more Southern states left the Union and joined the Confederacy: Virginia, Tennessee, Arkansas, and North Carolina. Four states would remain neutral throughout the Civil War: Maryland, Kentucky, Missouri, and Delaware. Altogether, the Confederacy was made up of eleven Southern states.

The first major battle between Union and Confederate military forces occurred in 1861 at the Battle of Bull Run. (The North named their battles after rivers, while Confederate forces named battles after nearby towns; therefore, the Confederates called Bull Run Manassas). Railroads played a key role in this battle, as General P. T. Beauregard was able to move his forces quickly to reinforce the Confederate forces and drive the Union forces from the battlefield. This is a strategy that Lincoln would not forget in future battles.

On September 17, 1862, an important battle occurred at Antietam (Confederates called it Sharpsburg) where more than 22,000 men were killed, wounded or missing in one day; it was the bloodiest day of battle in American history. Out of this bloody battle, Lincoln would formulate his Emancipation Proclamation, which would free the slaves in the southern states of rebellion (which would certainly not honor it) and leave enslaved the slaves in the border states such as Maryland, Kentucky, Missouri, and Delaware. This proclamation act was important, it led, after the war, to the abolition of slavery in the United States with the passage of the 13th Amendment to the Constitution in 1865.

The next two key battles of the war occurred in Vicksburg, Mississippi, and Gettysburg, Pennsylvania. Both battles would end on the Fourth of July 1863. The Battle of Vicksburg was led by an army under the command of General Ulysses S. Grant, who laid siege to Vicksburg for forty- six days. With the surrender of their fort, the Southern Confederacy was split in half, with the Union Navy and other military forces controlling the Mississippi River from Vicksburg in the state of Mississippi in the West.

At Gettysburg, Union forces led by General George Meade were able to stop Confederate forces in a three-day battle (July 1-July 3, 1863), which resulted in over 50,000 casualties on both sides. This was horrific battle, but it did stop Southern forces from penetrating the North and it led to the slow demise of the Confederacy. (Over one hundred years later, the U.S. military forces would lose over 50,000 men in the Vietnam War(1965-1973), but this was a war fought over several years and not one battle!

After the battle at Gettysburg, President Lincoln was invited to speak at the dedication of the battlefield a few months later, and wrote his stirring Gettysburg Address, which in just a few sentences summed up the enormous sacrifice of the army and helped put the battle in perspective for the American public.

In the Fall of 1864, Union forces led by General William Tecumseh Sherman pushed into the South from Chattanooga and eventually took over Atlanta in September 1864, ensuring the re-election of Abraham Lincoln in November 1864. In November 1864, Sherman also began his infamous March to the Sea, where he dropped his army from 100,000 men to approximately 60,000 men. This army lived off the land and marched across northern Georgia starting in Atlanta, burning the richest farmland in Georgia on a sixty-mile front, over 225 miles long, destroying everything in their path so the Confederacy couldn't use it to re-arm or replenish their supplies. This bold maneuver left many in the army's path to starve.

While this fighting went on in the southeastern part of the Confederacy, Grant led another Union army, laying siege to the Confederate capitol of Richmond, Virginia for over nine months. Eventually, in April 1865, Lee was forced to retreat, because he no longer had the manpower or the arms to protect Richmond against Union forces.

When an enemy invades your capital, the retreating army can declare the city an open city and hope that the invader does not burn it down (as the French government did with Paris in 1940) or you can burn it down and deny the invader use of your homes and buildings and other resources when they come into the area.

The retreating confederates decided on the scorched-earth policy, but ultimately this did not help them because the Union forces had them surrounded. Robert E. Lee finally surrendered to Grant at the Appomattox Court House on April 9, 1865. The one Confederate army left was commanded by General Joseph E. Johnston. Johnston surrendered to the Union General Sherman on April 26, 1865 in North Carolina. For many years afterward, April 26 was celebrated as Confederate Memorial Day.

Sadly, Abraham Lincoln did not live to see the last moments of the war. Five days after Lee surrendered to Grant, he was shot by actor John Wilkes Booth on April 14th, 1865 at Ford's Theater while watching a play entitled "Our American Cousin". Though fatally injured, Lincoln did not die until the next morning, April 15, 1865.

With Lincoln's assassination came a new president, a man wholly unfit for the office. Vice-President Andrew Johnson of Tennessee became President with Lincoln's last breath on April 15, 1865.

The total casualties for the Civil War, both Union and Confederate, of men killed, wounded or missing in action, were 1,084,938. The losses were staggering, and because Americans populated the armies of both sides, it is by far the largest loss of life we have suffered in any war or conflict, before or since. A generation of men never came home from the war.

The U.S. population in 1861 was over 31,000,000 people. The U.S. population today (2018) is over 324,000,000 people. To appreciate the Civil War losses in today's terms, you'd have to multiply the casualties by ten times, about 10,849,380 people lost, to compare with today's population.

Abraham Lincoln 16th President of the United States (March 4, 1861 to April 15, 1865)

http://cdn.loc.gov/service/pnp/cph/3a20000/3a24000/3a24100/3a24130r.jpg

The 17th President: Andrew Johnson

Andrew Johnson was the 17th President of the United States (April 15, 1865- March 4, 1869).

Born: December 9, 1808

Raleigh, N.C.

Died: July 31, 1875 (aged 66)

Near Carter Station, Tennessee

Education: No college education

Political Party Affiliation: Democrat

When Andrew Johnson became President with Lincoln's death on April 15, 1865, he inherited a political mess. The Radical Republican leaders like Charles Sumner and Thaddeus Stevens wanted to punish the American South for starting the war and killing their president.

However, within a short period, President Johnson pardoned about 13,000 former high-ranking Confederate office holders and military personnel. (As part of their legal deal, former high-ranking Confederate officials had to come to Washington D.C. to be pardoned *in person* by the President to become U.S. citizens again). President Johnson also announced that since former Confederate leaders had been pardoned and the former Confederate states had changed back their state constitutions to include the recommendations that he had made, Reconstruction was officially over.

The Radical Republicans were furious with President Johnson for finishing with Reconstruction, even as they wanted the chance to punish the South. Lincoln had been willing to re-admit 10% of the office holders who had voted for secession back into the Union; he had felt that would be enough. However, the Wade-Davis Bill created in 1864 would require 50 percent of the electorate that voted to secede in 1861 to vote for the former Confederate states to return to the Union.

President Johnson and the Radical Republicans conspired and voted against each other on legislation like the Freedman's Bureau, created to help the freed blacks and poor whites; Johnson vetoed the legislation. Congress then overrode his veto and created the Bureau. In fact, Johnson vetoed congressional legislation twenty-nine times; the Congress overrode his vetoes fifteen times.

In 1866, several southern states passed statutes called the black codes. Some of these codes seemed reminiscent of slavery; blacks could not own firearms or property, and in states like Mississippi, if they had not signed a labor contract by a certain time of the year, for example by the end of January, they could be put on a pedestal and their labor sold to the highest bidder for that year. This legislative act angered many northern Congressmen.

In 1866, the South also elected several former high-ranking Confederate leaders, including Alexander Stephens, the former vice-president of the Southern Confederacy. The northern Congressmen refused to seat these former Confederate officials by literally *locking them out of Congress*.

By 1867, the U.S. Congress (Northerners) got so incensed that they divided the American South (ten states in all) into five military districts, with each district having its own military governor.

The American South under Martial Law

Georgia's military governor was John Pope. When Georgia's political elite refused to have black office holders in the then-capital of Milledgeville, Pope moved the capital to Atlanta in 1868. During this time (1868-1870), the South was forced to accept the Fourteenth and Fifteenth Amendments to the Constitution. The Fourteenth Amendment gave citizenship to the former slaves, and equal protection under the law; the Fifteenth Amendment gave freed slaves the right to vote. Georgia officially returned to the Union in 1872. Some states, such as South Carolina, Florida, and Louisiana, were not permitted to return to the Union until 1877.

The Impeachment Trial of Andrew Johnson

President Johnson's constant bickering and fighting with the U.S. Congress turned many Congressmen against the president and led them to support the Radical Republican policies. Eventually, the House of Representatives enacted eleven impeachment statutes, which included the directive that he could not fire a member of his cabinet without Senate approval if the president selected and appointed him. This was the Office of Tenure Act of 1867. Many people felt it was unconstitutional, and it really didn't apply to Johnson, who did not appoint his Cabinet but inherited it from Lincoln. But the bill passed through Congress anyway. When Johnson vetoed it, Congress promptly overrode the veto.

This statute referred to one cabinet member. President Johnson fired Edwin Stanton, Secretary of War, because whatever Johnson said in a cabinet meeting, Stanton would turn around and report to the Radical Republicans. Johnson replaced Stanton temporarily with General Grant.

This should not have been a problem; Johnson's lawyer pointed out that President Lincoln had appointed Stanton to the Cabinet, not Johnson, which did not violate the Office of Tenure law. However, Radical Republicans such as Thaddeus Stevens and Charles Sumner sensed political weakness with President Johnson, and they moved in for the political kill through an impeachment trial. (Stanton's response to being fired was to barricade himself in his office for two months.)

The impeachment trial of the president began in March 1868 and lasted for three months. At the end, thirty-six senators needed to vote to remove President Johnson from office; thirty-five voted to remove him. One of the senators who had tremendous pressure put on him to vote for impeachment was Edmond Ross of Kansas; he refused to cave in to the Radical Republicans.

After this narrow escape, President Johnson kept a low profile until the end of his term. One notable achievement was the purchase of the land that became the state of Alaska from Russia during his term.

Johnson quietly left the White House and returned to Tennessee when Ulysses S. Grant was sworn in on March 4, 1869.

Andrew Johnson 17th President of the United States (April 15, 1865 to March 4, 1868)

http://cdn.loc.gov/service/pnp/cph/3a50000/3a53000/3a53200/3a53290r.jpg

The 18th President: Ulysses S. Grant

Ulysses Simpson Grant was the 18th President of the United States (March 4, 1869-March 4, 1877).

Born: April 27, 1822

Point Pleasant, Ohio

Died: July 23, 1885 (aged 63)

Mount McGregor, New York

Education: The Military Academy (West Point) (Graduated 1843)

Political Party Affiliation: Republican

President Ulysses Grant inherited a Reconstruction mess from Johnson, since the South was still under military occupation, and there was also the unfinished process of trying to create a system for the Freedmen to vote. Grant had an added incentive to help the Freedmen vote; it was their votes that won him the presidency.

The Ku Klux Klan was created in 1866 in Pulaski, Tennessee. It used terrorist tactics like beatings and lynchings to prevent the freedmen and white Republicans from creating working reconstructed governments in the South. Grant infiltrated the Klan in Texas in 1872 and used federal agents ruthlessly to break it up.

"Black Friday" Gold Scandal

President Grant suffered several scandals during his administration. His brother-in-law, Abel Corbin, and investors Jay Gould and Jim Fisk tried to corner the gold market. This trio of thieves drove up the price of gold. A $100.00 gold piece sold for $132.00 in greenbacks. However, by the latter part of September 1869, the price of gold was skyrocketing.

By September 23, 1869, $100.00 gold was worth $144.00 in greenbacks. The next day, September 24th, gold prices had risen again; one $100.00 gold piece was now worth $160.00 in greenbacks!

Grant realized what was happening, and he released the gold reserves from the Treasury ($4-million altogether) to make sure gold prices did not skyrocket any higher. This was known as the "Black Friday" gold scandal. The U.S. plunged into a great depression, which took years to recover from; this event really hurt the prestige of Grant's administration.

The Credit Mobilier Scandal 1872-1873

The stockholders of the Union Pacific Railroad created a new railroad company in 1872, the Credit Mobilier of America, and they sold shares to prominent politicians. These politicians were members of the U.S. Congress, so they awarded Credit Mobilier lucrative subsidies and did not pay attention to business expenses. Many of the original investors made large profits. When the scandal broke, several well-known politicians were discovered to have been involved; this included Schuyler Colfax, the outgoing vice-president of Grant's first administration. James G. Blaine, the Republican candidate for president in 1884, was also involved. James Garfield, who became president in 1880, was involved, too.

Failure of Western Towns to Keep Up with Railroad Expansion

An economic depression occurred in 1873, because the U.S. government had opened the transcontinental railroad when the East and West had finally been connected at Promontory Point, Utah in 1869. Many western towns which were built around these railroad hubs were expected to flourish, but they did not. Population growth was slower than expected, because the pioneers had taken longer than expected to move out to these locations. Also, more people in a population means more food and supplies are necessary to sustain them. This means more cargo must ship, both East and West, along the rail lines. When the expected income did not materialize as expected, many banks failed nationwide.

While Grant remained a military hero, his presidency was not considered a success.

Ulysses Grant 18th President of the United States
http://cdn.loc.gov/service/pnp/pga/12900/12917v.jpg

The 19th President: Rutherford Hayes

Rutherford Hayes was the 19th President of the United States (March 4, 1877-March 4, 1881).

Born: October 4, 1822

Delaware, Ohio

Died: January 17, 1893 (aged 70)

Fremont, Ohio

Education: Kenton College: Bachelor's degree; Harvard Law School: Bachelor of Law;

Political Party Affiliation: Republican

The 1876 would be another contested presidential election.

The Democratic candidate was Samuel J. Tilden of New York while the Republican candidate was Rutherford Hayes. This was at the end of the Reconstruction Period. There were still three southern states with federal troops within their respective borders: South Carolina, Florida, and Louisiana.

When the electoral votes for the election came back to Washington D.C., there were two separate electoral votes: one set for Samuel J. Tilden, the other for Rutherford Hayes. The Democratic nominee Tilden had 184 electoral votes. A candidate needed 185 to win. So he needed one electoral vote while the Republican nominee Hayes needed all twenty remaining electoral votes to win.

Since the U.S. Constitution did not allow for two separate electoral votes Congress had to appoint a special committee to look at these votes. The Democrat challenger Samuel Tilden also won the popular votes too: he had 4,300,590 to Hayes' 4,036,298.

The final tally of electoral votes was 185 for Rutherford Hayes, 184 for Samuel Tilden.

A committee was created to decide what to do about the electoral votes, with eight Republicans, seven Democrats. The group voted along party lines and now, the Republican candidate Rutherford Hayes acquired all twenty necessary electoral votes and became president. Immediately, Democrats cried that the Republicans had stolen the election and that there should be civil unrest, even if this led to another civil war.

The two parties worked out their differences with the Compromise of 1877:

(1) The Republican party would retain the presidency and remain a national party.

(2) The Democratic party would stay a more local and regional political party, especially in the South, where they became a white supremacist party. The Republican party would leave them alone to govern their own affairs in the South.

(3) The South would be rebuilt, and railroads, canals, and other infrastructure that had been damaged during the Civil War would be repaired.

(4) The last federal troops would be pulled out of the South as well.

(5) In return for all this, Hayes agreed to serve only one term as president.

Rutherford Hayes 19th President of the United States (March 4, 1877 to March 4, 1881)
http://cdn.loc.gov/service/pnp/cph/3a50000/3a53000/3a53200/3a53292r.jpg

The 20th President: James Garfield

James Garfield was the 20th President of the United States (March 4, 1881-September 19, 1881).

Born: November 19, 1831

Cuyahoga County, Ohio

Died: September 19, 1881 (aged 49)

Long Branch, New Jersey

Education: Williams College. Bachelor's degree

Political Party Affiliation: Republican

President Garfield did not have time to do much with his Administration, because he was assassinated six months into his Administration by Charles Guiteau, who had wanted to be named Garfield's ambassador to France and was disappointed. He shot at Garfield as he and James Blaine, who had run for president against him as the Republican senator from Maine, walked through a Washington train station.

President Garfield did not die immediately from his wound, but lingered for several weeks and conducted government business, in terrible pain, from his bed. (He was shot on July 2, 1881, but he did not die until September 19, 1881). The doctors kept probing his body for the bullet, using dirty hands and unclean instruments, and when he had a heart attack, they diagnosed it improperly. After he died, the bullet was found in a protective cyst near his spine. If the doctors had left him alone, Garfield very likely would have lived. When he died, Vice-President Chester Arthur became the new President of the

United States. Garfield's assassin Charles Guiteau was executed on June 30, 1882.

James Garfield 20th President of the United States (March 4, 1881 to September 19, 1881)
http://cdn.loc.gov/service/pnp/cph/3a50000/3a53000/3a53200/3a53293r.jpg

The 21st President: Chester A. Arthur

Chester Alan Arthur was the 21st President of the United States (September 19, 1881-March 4, 1885).

Born: October 5, 1829

Fairfield, Vermont

Died: November 18, 1886 (aged 57)

Manhattan, New York

Education: Union College and State and National Law School (he did not graduate).

Political Party Affiliation: Republican

Like President John Tyler, Arthur's predecessor died while in office, and he assumed office in the middle of his predecessor's term. Once Arthur became president, however, he did not appoint a vice-president.

Chester Arthur's greatest achievement as president was the passage of the Pendleton Act of 1883.

This act, the first of its kind in civil-service reform, guaranteed that civil servants could not be automatically fired every time whenever a new presidential administration began, but could retain their jobs if they were qualified for them. Federal bureaucrats were tested to prove they knew their jobs, and kept their jobs based on merit, not party affiliation. (It is ironic that Arthur would support reform legislation, between 1871 and 1878, since he had been the tax collector of the port of New York where corruption was rampant.) The Brooklyn Bridge was also completed in 1883, while he was president. President Arthur also began the process of modernizing the U.S. Navy.

No one knew throughout his Administration that Arthur had Bright's Disease, a fatal kidney disease.

But two years after leaving office, he died, at the age of fifty-seven.

Chester Arthur 21st President of the United States (September 19, 1881, to March 4, 1885)
http://cdn.loc.gov/service/pnp/cph/3a50000/3a53000/3a53200/3a53294v.jpg

The 22nd President: Grover Cleveland

Grover Cleveland was the 22nd (and later, the 24th) President of the United States (March 4, 1885-

March 4, 1889).

Born: March 18, 1837

Caldwell, New Jersey

Died: June 24, 1908 (aged 71)

Princeton, New Jersey

Education. No college education; however, he did become a lawyer after completing an apprenticeship

with a lawyer.

Political Party Affiliation: Democrat

The Presidential Election of 1884

Cleveland has been the only president, so far, to serve two non-consecutive terms as president.

Cleveland's 1884 presidential election was close; he narrowly defeated Maine Senator James G. Blaine,

219 to 182 electoral votes. Cleveland also beat Blaine in the popular vote, by 23,000 votes.

Grover Cleveland was the first Democrat elected as President of the United States since James

Buchanan, in 1856. (Andrew Johnson was a Democrat, but he was not elected; he became president when Lincoln was assassinated.) New York, a swing state, gave Cleveland the edge when he won the state's 36 electoral votes. Cleveland, who had been mayor of Buffalo and then governor of New York, was honest and interested in reform, in stark contrast to the corruption of Tammany Hall, an infamous New York political machine, known for taking bribes and graft for decades.

Cleveland, who believed in limited government, blocked pensions for Civil War veterans which he believed were fraudulent. He also supported keeping the gold standard for American money, and lowering tariffs, which eventually cost him re-election in 1888. Meanwhile, in two terms in office, Cleveland vetoed more bills than all previous presidents before him *combined*. He set the standard for upcoming twentieth-century presidents and their more active role in governing.

Grover Cleveland 22nd President of the United States
(March 4, 1885 to March 4, 1889)
http://cdn.loc.gov/service/pnp/cph/3a50000/3a53000/3a53200/3a53295r.jpg

The 23rd President: Benjamin Harrison

Benjamin Harrison was the 23rd President of the United States (March 4, 1889-March 4, 1893).

Born: August 20, 1833

North Bend, Ohio

Died: March 13, 1901 (aged 67)

Indianapolis, Indiana

Political Party Affiliation: Republican

The Presidential Election of 1888

Harrison defeated Cleveland in the electoral college (233 to 168), though Cleveland did beat him by 100,000 votes in the popular vote. Thus, Benjamin Harrison, grandson of President William Henry Harrison, became president in 1889.

President Harrison was another president who built up the U.S. Navy; since countries like Great Britain, France, Germany, and Japan had strong Navies, President Harrison realized that the U.S. would need a strong Navy to compete with them. He also supported the McKinley Tariff of 1890, which placed a large tariff on imported goods, allowing American manufactured goods to compete with foreign goods. President Harrison also started a movement to preserve land for national parks in places such as Yosemite and Sequoia National Parks in California.

It was also during his presidency that Ellis Island was built (1892) to help process newly-arrived foreigners coming to America. While it was in operation, Ellis Island processed millions of immigrants.

Harrison signed the 1890 Sherman Antitrust Act, to limit monopolies in American business.

However, many legislative actions by President Harrison would have important consequences for future presidents, such as Theodore Roosevelt. However, his actions did not particularly benefit him during his presidency, and he was not re-elected in 1892.

Benjamin Harrison 23rd President of the United States
March 4, 1889 to March 4, 1893)
http://cdn.loc.gov/service/pnp/cph/3a00000/3a02000/3a02200/3a02269v.jpg

The 24th President: Grover Cleveland

Grover Cleveland was the 24th (as well as the 22nd) President of the United States (March 4, 1893-March 4, 1897). This was the second of his non-consecutive terms as president.

Born: March 18, 1837

Caldwell, New Jersey

Died: June 24, 1908 (aged 71)

Princeton, New Jersey

Education: No college education. However, he became a lawyer by doing an apprenticeship with an established lawyer. (He was 22 years old when he passed the bar).

Political Party Affiliation: Democrat

The Presidential Election of 1892

Grover Cleveland became president by beating Benjamin Harrison in the electoral college with 277 votes to Harrison's 145 electoral votes. Cleveland also won the popular vote by more than 400,000 votes.

Most of Cleveland's noteworthy accomplishments occurred during his second term. The President believed in classical liberalism, which today means libertarianism, or very limited government. The Wilson-Gorman Tariff of 1894 got rid of tariffs on iron ore, coal, lumber and wool, which Cleveland supported. However, once changes were made to the bill, which nullified most of the provisions and added a version of an income tax, Cleveland was furious. He refused to sign the bill, but it became law without his signature. In 1895, the income-tax part of the law was struck down by the Supreme Court.

Cleveland also vetoed a bill that would pay pensions to members of the Grand Army of the

Republic, which had fought for the Union during the Civil War. In fact, except for Franklin Delano Roosevelt, Cleveland vetoed more congressional legislation than any other president (414) In 1887, he signed into law a bill creating the Interstate Commerce Commission to regulate the rates that the railroads charged its customers—both people and towns. President Cleveland is the only president to marry while in the White House: He married Frances Folsom on June 2, 1886. Mrs. Folsom was 21 years old at the time of their wedding; President Cleveland was 48 years old.

President Cleveland also strengthened the coastal defenses of the United States against a foreign Navy by putting more gun batteries facing out toward the sea. He modernized the U.S. Navy by building more steel ships. In fact, President Cleveland had sixteen steel warships built that would prove vital during the Spanish-American War of 1898.

Cleveland also revoked the Sherman Silver Purchase Act of 1890, which required the U.S. government to purchase a certain amount of silver every month. He took a broad interpretation of the Monroe Doctrine, saying that when a border dispute happened in 1895 between British Guiana and Venezuela, the matter had to be taken to court for arbitration.

Cleveland also recognized the Republic of Hawaii in 1894. The U.S. government had intended to annex Hawaii in 1893 but Cleveland withdrew from that treaty when he learned that not only did most Hawaiians feel strongly against annexation, but the queen of Hawaii was overthrown by a group that included the current U.S. Ambassador to Hawaii. When the provisional government in Hawaii refused to leave there under direct orders, Cleveland did not send in troops to enforce his will.

In 1893, a low in the gold reserves caused a financial panic; Cleveland ordered the sale of

government bonds for gold and silver, which brought in many millions to the treasury. The economy did not completely improve until the end of his term. In 1896, the Plessy vs. Ferguson Supreme Court decision led to decades of legal segregation in the black community, if their facilities were considered 'separate but equal' to those of white people.

Grover Cleveland 24th President of the United States
    (March 4, 1893 to March 4, 1897)
        http://cdn.loc.gov/service/pnp/cph/3a50000/3a53000/3a53200/3a53295r.jpg

The 25th President: William McKinley

William McKinley was the 25th President of the United States (March 4, 1896-Sept 6, 1901).

Born: January 29, 1843

Niles, Ohio

Died: September 6, 1901 (aged 58)

Buffalo, New York

Education: Albany Law School; earned a law degree.

Political Party Affiliation: Republican

The Presidential Election of 1896

The presidential election of 1896 between the Republican candidate, William McKinley, and the Democrat William Jennings Bryan was one of the most contested elections ever, with the merging industrial power of the East and the Midwest opposing the agrarian power of the South and the West. William Jennings Bryan was the frontrunner of the Democratic party, which favored the free coinage of silver, a policy supported by farmers in the South and the West, because they believed that with coinage exchanged both in silver and gold, the additional silver would increase inflation, and farmers would be able to earn more money for their crops, with inflation also driving down the costs of their debts, too. Jennings became so passionate in his campaign speeches that he routinely enthralled audiences with his final sentence: "You shall not crucify mankind upon a cross of gold!"

The Populist, or People's, party believed in the free coinage of silver too, but that is about the only thing that they agreed with William Jennings Bryan on. However, they were afraid that if the populists ran as a third party, this would split the Democratic vote and hand the election to William McKinley and the Republicans. The Populists decided to join the Democrats in the presidential election, with their candidate, Tom Watson, running for vice-president.

William McKinley ran a front-porch campaign, where other people (by some estimates as many as 1400 people) traveled across the country to speak for him. His campaign manager, Mark Hanna, spent more money on this one election than all previous presidential elections. McKinley and Hanna played on the fears of the business community, that if Jennings and the populists won, it would lead to communism and the loss of their business and private property.

The result was that voters voted in record numbers (80 percent or higher). Still, McKinley won twenty-three states vote while Jennings won twenty-two. McKinley beat Jennings in the electoral college 271 to 176; McKinley also won the popular vote by 600,000 votes. Many historians believe that Mark Hanna and William McKinley were able to scare the emerging middle class into believing that the Democrats and especially the populists wanted to destroy private enterprise and create class warfare. Whether it was true or not, it worked.

The Spanish-American War of 1898

When the *U.S.S. Maine*, a premiere battleship in the U.S. Navy, was sent to Cuba as part of a naval exercise and mysteriously blew up in Havana Harbor on February 15, 1898, killing all 268 men on board, Americans were outraged.

To this day, opinions are divided on why the *Maine* exploded. Some scholars claim that it was problems with the storage of gunpowder in the ship's magazines, that an accidental spark then led to an explosion. Other journalists of the time said that Spanish anarchists had blown up the ship because they were offended that the ship was in Cuban waters, and Cuba was a Spanish possession at the time.

A popular jingo during the Spanish-American War was, "Remember the *Maine*, to hell with Spain!"

After the *Maine* sank, events between the U.S. and Spain reached critical mass rapidly:

April 11, 1898: After talking to his Secretary of War, John Hays, and other cabinet members, President McKinley decides to go to war with Spain.

April 24: Spain goes to war with the U.S. after diplomacy fails.

April 25: The U.S. Congress declares war on Spain.

May 1, 1898: In the Battle of Manila Bay, the Spanish Pacific naval fleet is destroyed.

July 1, 1898: With U.S. troops now fighting in Cuba, Future President Theodore Roosevelt charges up San Juan Hill with his group of Rough Riders, which shortens the war and makes Theodore Roosevelt a national hero.

July 17, 1898: The city of Santiago, Cuba surrenders to U.S. General William Shafter.

August 12, 1898: Spain agrees to grant Cuba independence and cede Puerto Rico and Guam to the U.S., ending the war between the two countries.

August 14, 1898: Spain surrenders to the U.S. in the Philippines.

December 10, 1898: The U.S. and Spain sign the Treaty of Paris, ending the Spanish-American War. The U.S. emerges as a new world power, with Asian colonies such as the Philippines and Guam, and in the Caribbean, Puerto Rico and Cuba.

In 1900, the Hay-Pauncefote Treaty, signed by Great Britain and the U.S., opened the way for the U.S. to build a canal in Central America. This would become the Panama Canal.

Also in 1900, McKinley signed the Gold Standard Act, which set gold as the standard for American money and ended the debate over gold- and silver-backed money. The Organic Act made Hawaii a U.S. territory. McKinley won re-election to a second term in November 1900 and was inaugurated the following March.

However, barely after his second term began, President McKinley was shot by Polish anarchist Leon Czolgosz on September 6, 1901, at the Pan-American Exposition in Buffalo, New York. He died of his wound a week later, and Vice President Theodore Roosevelt became the 26th president.

William McKinley 25th President of the United States (March 4, 1897 to September 14, 1901)
http://cdn.loc.gov/service/pnp/cph/3a50000/3a53000/3a53200/3a53298v.jpg

The 26th President: Theodore Roosevelt

Theodore Roosevelt was the 26th President of the United States (1901-1909).

Born: October 27, 1858

New York, New York

Died: January 6, 1919 (aged 60)

Oyster Bay, New York

Education: Harvard University: Bachelor's degree;

Political Party Affiliation: Republican

Theodore Roosevelt (hereafter referred to as T.R.) was one of the most energetic presidents in American history. Before he was president, he was a New York State Assemblyman, Assistant Secretary of the Navy and Governor of New York. He became famous for leading a charge up San Juan Hill during the Spanish-American War. T.R. led a group called the "Rough Riders"; he and his men helped end the war in Cuba, because with their famous charge, they weakened Spanish forces on the island.

In fact, T.R. was posthumously awarded the medal of honor in 2001 for his actions in Cuba. T.R. was also the governor of New York in 1898; President McKinley picked him to be his vice-presidential candidate in the election of 1900. Upon President McKinley's death in September 1901, T.R. became the new president; at the age of forty-two, he was the youngest man to become president up to that time. T.R. averted a national emergency when he intervened in the coal strike negotiations of 1902. A potential strike would have meant that millions of people would not have had coal to heat their homes in winter. The striking coal miners wanted a pay raise of 20 percent and shorter working hours.

T.R. set up a meeting with the strikers and the business owners, and they reached an agreement. The coal mine owners agreed to a 10 percent wage increase. Their work day was reduced from ten to nine hours. In return, the miners agreed that the owners did not have to recognize a miners' union.

Although the Interstate Commerce Commission had been created in 1887, during the Harrison administration, T.R. used it to pass two rules: The Elkins Act of 1903 imposed heavy fines on railroads who offered rebates (kickbacks) to shippers that struck unofficial deals with them. The Hepburn Act of 1906 gave the ICC the power to regulate the maximum shipping rates that railroads could charge. This was a way for T.R. to control the monopolistic power of the railroads.

T.R. also controlled the beef industry, when it became clear that certain meat companies were colluding to set higher prices, to make bigger profits. In 1906, Congress passed the Pure Food and Drug Act, which laid the foundation for the creation of the Food and Drug Administration (FDA). The Meat Inspection Act was passed to protect the American public from tainted food.

T.R. also signed a bill creating five national parks, 150 national forests, and the U.S. Forest Service. He supported a group of revolutionaries in present-day Panama when this group declared its independence from Colombia; he sent U.S. warships into the area, setting in motion the later creation of the Panama Canal. The leaders of this group signed a peace treaty with the U.S. in 1904, and ten years later, in 1914, the Panama Canal was opened. T.R. also strengthened the U.S. navy while he was president. He was awarded the Nobel Peace Prize in 1906 for negotiating an end to the Russo-Japanese War of 1905.

Theodore Roosevelt 26th President of the United States
(September 14, 1901 to March 4, 1909)
http://cdn.loc.gov/service/pnp/ppmsca/35600/35652v.jpg

The 27th President: William Taft

William Howard Taft was the 27th President of the United States (March 4, 1909-March 4, 1913).

Born: September 15, 1857

Cincinnati, Ohio

Died: March 8, 1930 (aged 72)

Washington, D.C.

Education: Yale University; Bachelor's degree; University of Cincinnati College of Law; Bachelor of

Law

Political Party Affiliation: Republican

Taft became the 27th president by beating the Democratic opponent, William Jennings Bryan, in the

electoral college, 321 votes to 162 votes. Theodore Roosevelt is famous for trust busting (breaking up

monopolies), but Taft busted more trusts: Taft launched 70 trust busts in four years while Theodore

Roosevelt launched 40 trust busts in seven years. One of the companies that President Taft had

launched a 'trust suit' against was the American Sugar Refining Company, which had colluded to get

higher prices for their product, costing American consumers more money.

Taft was the first president to throw out a first pitch at a baseball game. He was the first president to

play golf. He was also the last U.S. President to have facial hair. Also, The 16th Amendment was added to the U.S. Constitution on February 3, 1913, during President Taft's administration, which for the first time in American history levied taxes on Americans' income. Taft was also the heaviest president, weighing in at over three hundred and fifty pounds. Because of his excess weight, he once got stuck in a bathtub in the White House and needed assistance to get out.

After his presidency ended, Taft was named Chief Justice of the U.S. Supreme Court (July 11, 1921-March 3, 1930). He is the only former president ever to be named to the U.S. Supreme Court as a justice.

82

William Howard Taft 27th President of the United States
(March 4, 1908 to March 4, 1913)
http://cdn.loc.gov/service/pnp/cph/3c00000/3c03000/3c03100/3c03185v.jpg

The Presidential Election of 1912

Woodrow Wilson (Democrat) won the 1912 presidential election, with 435 electoral votes. Theodore Roosevelt (Progressive), who ran independently, after 7 ½ years as president previously, won 88 electoral votes. William H. Taft (Republican), running for re-election, won 8 electoral votes. Eugene V. Debs (Socialist) won 0 votes. Wilson easily won the 1912 presidential election, because when Theodore Roosevelt failed to win the Republican nomination over Taft, he formed a third party, the Progressive Party, better known as the Bull Moose party. By taking this action, Roosevelt split the Republican party's popular and electoral votes, and Wilson, former president of Princeton University in New Jersey, won the presidency.

The Presidential Election of 1916

President Woodrow Wilson (Democrat) won re-election in the 1916 presidential election, with 277 electoral votes; his Republican opponent, Charles E. Hughes, won 254 electoral votes and Allan Benson (Socialist) won 0 electoral votes. Wilson's campaign slogan in 1916 was, "He kept us out of war." However, by April 6, 1917, the U.S. would be at war with Germany, the first of two world wars it would fight against Germany in the 20th century.

The 28th President: Woodrow Wilson

Woodrow Wilson was the 28th President of the United States (March 4, 1913-March 4, 1921).

Born: December 8, 1856

Staunton, Va.

Died: February 3, 1924 (aged 67)

Washington, D.C.

Education: Princeton University: Bachelor's degree; John Hopkins University: Doctoral degree

Political Party Affiliation: Democrat

Constitutional Amendments Passed

Wilson's presidency was unusual, in that three constitutional amendments were passed during his two terms in office.

The 17th Amendment was ratified by the United States Congress on May 13, 1913, which led to direct election of U.S. Senators by the American voters and not by their State legislatures. Before the 17th Amendment, state legislatures in each state chose the two people to serve their state in the United States Senate. The 18th Amendment (Prohibition) prohibited the manufacture, sale, and distribution of alcohol within the United States. The 18th amendment was ratified by U.S. Congress on January 29, 1919. The 19th amendment, giving women the right to vote, was ratified on August 18, 1920 by the U.S. Congress.

Federal Government Agencies Created During Wilson's Presidency

The Federal Reserve Act was signed by President Woodrow Wilson on December 13, 1913. This created the Federal Reserve System, which effectively became the central banking system of the United States. This system gave authority to the Federal Reserve to issue Federal Reserve Notes (U.S. dollars).

The Federal Trade Commission Act, created on September 1914, is a five-member board that oversees business practices in the U.S., to ensure that no unfair business practices defraud the American public, and to punish those that do.

The Federal Farm Loan Act of 1916 gave credit to farmers in rural areas in the United States, which allowed farmers to compete with big business.

The Federal Clayton Antitrust Act of 1914 defined criminal acts for the chief officers of the corporate offices and clarified guidelines for the corporations.

Laws passed

The Smith-Lever Act of 1914 taught American farmers how to increase their crop output with the latest advances in farming techniques. The Adamson Act (1916) reduced railroad workers' hours to eight hours per day, and paid overtime for extra hours of work. This is important, because railroads were threatening a nationwide strike.

Mexican revolutionary Francisco "Pancho" Villa attacked Columbus, New Mexico, on March 9, 1916; he and his followers killed 19 people and burned the town down. President Wilson sent U.S. military forces to chase Villa in Mexico. Six thousand soldiers, led by General John Pershing, chased

Villa for two years, but even though they had several skirmishes with Villa's men, they were unable to capture him, though they did kill 120 Mexican guerrillas on either side of the border.

Wilson's first wife Ellen Axson Wilson died in 1914 of a liver condition; in 1915 he married Edith Bolling Galt, a strong-willed widow. When Wilson suffered a stroke in 1919 and became partially paralyzed, Edith took over many of his responsibilities in government and exerted tremendous influence over his time and decisions.

World War I

In January 1917, British code breakers broke the code that the Germans used during World War I. These British code breakers intercepted a telegram sent by the German foreign secretary, Arthur Zimmerman, to the German ambassador to Mexico, Heinrich von Eckardt. The telegram proposed a deal in the event of war between Germany and the United States: The German ambassador would offer Mexican authorities the land that was taken from them during the Mexican-American War (which comprised the states of Arizona, California, Texas, and New Mexico).

British authorities did not release this information immediately, because they did not want to alert German authorities to the fact that they had deciphered their code. The British presented the Zimmerman telegram to President Woodrow Wilson on February 24, 1917. Wilson turned the information over to the newspapers on March 1, 1917. The political firestorm created by this document was one of the reasons why the U.S. declared war on Germany.

Unrestricted submarine warfare was another major cause of World War I.

During World War I, Britain had the strongest Navy in the world; Germany could not compete with Britain at sea, because they had to maintain a large army; there were military threats from France to the west and Russia to the east. They chose instead to use the submarine, Unterseeboot (in German), or more popularly, the U-boat.

The only way the U-boat could offset British naval supremacy was to sink every vessel believed to be a British warship, and this they did, using unrestricted submarine warfare, where German U-boats sank armed ships without warning, but tried to avoid passenger ships.

There were saboteurs everywhere. On May 7, 1915, the British passenger liner *Lusitania* was torpedoed by a German U-boat. Counting passengers and crew, nearly 2,000 people were on board and since the ship sank so quickly, 1,200 people drowned, including 128 Americans. President Wilson sent a strongly-worded telegram to German authorities that if Germany did not curtail such actions, it could possibly lead to war between Germany and the United States. Germany apologized but claimed the ship was carrying munitions and therefore was not a neutral ship, and it might have been, which would explain why it sank so quickly.

Germany also sank the French passenger ship *Sussex* on March 26, 1916. (The Sussex had 80 casualties, including two Americans). President Wilson then threatened to break diplomatic ties with Germany, which is usually the first step before countries declare war on each other.

This prompted the German Government on May 1, 1916, to announce that it would back off on unrestricted submarine warfare. This pledge held until February 1917, when Germany announced that it would resume unrestricted submarine warfare. It was a number of these incidents that turned public sentiment in favor of war with Germany. President Wilson went to Congress for a declaration of war on April 2, 1917. By April 6, 1917, both houses of Congress had declared war on Germany.

In August 1914, the Western Front emerged, which stretched 475 miles from the top at the North Sea to its southern limits at the Swiss border. The principal combatants were France, Russia (until 1917), and Great Britain, who were the Allies. Their enemies were the Germans and Austro-Hungarians, known as the Central Powers.

By the time that Germany announced it would renew unrestricted submarine warfare, Germany hoped to knock both France and Great Britain out of the war. Using submarine warfare, the Germans hoped to sink all the British ships; within three months of the start of the submarine offensive, May 1917, the Germans had sunk so many British ships that the British Isles only had food on hand to last six weeks. (Britain had to import its food because it could not produce enough on the British Isles).

The Germans hoped to knock both the French and the British out of the war before America's military might could become a factor. The Germans officially ended their war with Russia on March 3, 1918, with the signing of the Treaty of Brest-Litovsk. Russia was undergoing its own civil Revolution and needed to focus its energy internally.

Now that the Eastern Front was over, the Germans could start moving their 50 divisions of troops (over 500,000 men) from the Eastern Front to the Western Front to attack France.

The German Spring Offensive (March 21, 1918 to July 18, 1918).

America was able to make its might felt in different ways. In the Battle of Cantigny, on May 28, 1918, American service men not only beat the German troops in the area. (with 4,000 troops in the battle) but they also withstood several German counterattacks. This proved that American soldiers can fight the Germans successfully, and gave the French and British troops more faith in the

American troops as well.

The Battle of Belleau Wood (June 1, 1918-June 26, 1918) was an important battle. Both French and American forces fought German military forces to a standstill. The battle cost the American military about 10,000 casualties, including those killed, wounded or missing in action. However, had the Germans been able to break through Allied forces at this point, the city of Paris lay only forty-five miles way.

One Hundred Day Offensive of the Allies of 1918

From July 18th until the armistice was signed on November 11, 1918, the Allies launched a counterattack, known as both the One Hundred Day Offensive and the second Battle of the Marne, in which the Allies, with fresh American troops, pushed the Germans out of France and into parts of Belgium. However, the German army was still technically in the field on November 11, 1918, when the Germans signed the armistice to stop fighting temporarily; the Germans and the Allies later signed the Treaty of Versailles in 1919, officially ending World War I. Two days before, Kaiser Wilhelm of Germany had abdicated his throne.

The greatest effect that new American troops had on the Allies was an uplift in morale. With about 10,000 fresh American troops arriving daily, and Germany and its allies already exhausted from four years of war, they could not match the kind of manpower that America mustered. By the end of World War I, over 320,000 U.S. military had been killed, wounded or were missing in action.

The League of Nations

President Woodrow Wilson helped create the League of Nations, the predecessor to the United Nations. This covenant of nations would, in theory, give nations of the world a place to go to resolve their differences without going to war. President Wilson also came up with the Fourteen Points document to end World War I.

Germany signed the Treaty of Versailles in 1919 thinking that France, Great Britain, and the United States would follow the guidelines outlined in Wilson's Fourteen Points, but the Allies, angry and bitter after a costly war, refused to follow them. (The League of Nations, #14 on Wilson's Fourteen Points, was the only part of his doctrine they agreed to.) The bitter terms of the Treaty of Versailles, with costly war reparations that would grind Germany down for a generation, humiliated Germany completely and led to the rise in the 1920's and 1930's of Adolf Hitler.

Woodrow Wilson won the Nobel Peace Prize in October 1919, for creating the League of Nations, which began at the Paris Peace Conference that ended the First World War. The U.S. Senate refused to ratify the Treaty of Versailles in 1919 because of opposition led by the Senate Leader Henry Cabot Lodge III. It was rejected again on March 19, 1920.

Woodrow Wilson 28th President of the United States
(March 4, 1913 to March 4, 1921)
http://cdn.loc.gov/service/pnp/cph/3a20000/3a21000/3a21700/3a21763v.jpg

The 29th President: Warren Harding

Warren Gamaliel (G.) Harding was the 29th President of the United States (March 4, 1921-August 2, 1923).

Born: November 2, 1865

Blooming Grove, Ohio

Died: August 2, 1923 (aged 57)

San Francisco, Ca.

Education: Ohio Central College: Bachelor's degree.

Warren G. Harding started a newspaper called the *Marion Star* in Marion, Ohio, which became successful before he entered politics. He went on to become a member of the state senate of Ohio in 1899, and later he became the Lieutenant Governor of Ohio. In 1914, he became a U.S. Senator. In 1920, he won a landslide election to become President.

Harding's Domestic Policy

President Harding passed the federal child welfare program. He lowered taxes, increased the tax base, and raised tariffs to create employment. He ended the railroad strike of Blair Mountain and the Railroad strike of 1922.

While Harding was very popular during his Administration for cutting taxes, raising tariffs and tightening immigration, corruption was lurking just below the surface. He did not live to face its fallout, however; while touring the country, he fell ill with ptomaine poisoning. (Ptomaine poisoning is the old-fashioned term used to describe food poisoning). He died in his hotel room in San Francisco on August 2, 1923.

After he died, in 1923, The Teapot Dome Scandal burst open. This was a scheme implicating Secretary of the Interior Albert Falls, whose control of naval oil reserves on public land in Teapot Dome, Wyoming and Elk Hills, California was absolute. Because of his greed, Falls accepted bribes from individual businessmen, amounting to $300,000, to lease those reserves to private oil interests. Falls ultimately went to jail for a year, but the scandal affected public opinion of the dead president. When in 1930 a woman named Nan Britton published a book claiming she was the mother of his illegitimate child, the scandals eroded Harding's popularity entirely.

Harding's Foreign Policy

At the Washington Naval Armament Conference (1921-1922), several countries agreed to reduce the size of their Navies in the 1920s: Great Britain and the United States kept theirs approximately the same size, as did Japan, France and Italy. The Washington Arms Treaty allowed certain countries to sink or sell their older ships and streamline their Navies to save money. The treaty lasted for ten years.

Warren Harding also signed separate peace treaties with both Austria and Germany, officially ending the state of war that existed between them during World War I, since the U.S. Senate had rejected the Treaty of Versailles.

Warren G. Harding 29th President of the United States
(March 4, 1921 to August 2, 1923)
http://cdn.loc.gov/service/pnp/cph/3b30000/3b37000/3b37800/3b37824r.jpg

The 30th President: Calvin Coolidge

Calvin Coolidge was the 30th President of the United States (August 2, 1923-March 4, 1929).

Born: July 4, 1872

Plymouth, Vermont

Died: January 5, 1933 (aged 60)

Northhampton, Massachusetts

Education: Amherst College: Bachelor's degree;

Political Party Affiliation: Republican

President Calvin Coolidge became president on the sudden death of President Warren Harding in 1923. Coolidge signed the Immigration Act of 1924, which tightened immigration quotas, a course that would continue until the 1960's.

Coolidge refused to hire members of the KKK for government positions, gave government jobs to blacks and granted citizenship rights to Native Americans. Now, Native Americans could remain in their country and had rights to tribal lands. Coolidge also lowered the national debt from 22.3 billion to 16.9 billion. At approximately the same time, the federal budget was lowered from 5.1 billion in 1921 to 3.3 billion in 1929. Coolidge had goals he wanted to achieve in his presidency. Having achieved them all, he announced he would not run for another term.

Calvin Coolidge 30th President of the United States
(August 2, 1923 to March 4, 1929)
http://cdn.loc.gov/service/pnp/cph/3a50000/3a53000/3a53300/3a53302v.jpg

The 31st President: Herbert Hoover

Herbert Hoover was the 31st President of the United States (March 4, 1929- March 4, 1933).

Born: August 10, 1874

West Branch, Iowa

Died: October 20, 1964 (aged 90)

New York City, New York

 Education: Stanford University: Bachelor's degree;

Political Party Affiliation: Republican

Hoover's Domestic Policy

Herbert Hoover, born to Quaker parents and orphaned as a young boy, was a millionaire who had managed the food conservation program very successfully during World War I, under President Wilson. He made his personal fortune as an engineer, with a belief in personal responsibility and a minimum of federal interference.

Hoover withdrew U.S. troops from Nicaragua and Haiti, increased federal funding to Howard University (a traditional black college), and supported the idea that share croppers and tenant farmers should have the opportunity to own the land that they worked on. He also supported more rights and better living conditions for Native Americans and increased the amount of land in the National Park Systems.

However, Hoover's presidency is best known for the start of the Great Depression, when the stock market crashed on October 29, 1929, effectively ending the Roaring Twenties, and wiping out the fortunes of many wealthy investors.

When Hoover, to bring relief to Americans, raised tariffs on foreign goods to limit competition for domestic goods, other countries did the same, and several exporters were ruined. The American economy worsened, the unemployment rate grew to 25 percent (25 million people out of work), men sold apples in the streets to eke out a living and poverty became part of many households. With no federal social safety-net programs in place, people began to go hungry. Industrial output for the U.S. fell by 50 percent and many Americans were not optimistic about the future.

Though the Great Depression started in America, it soon spread to such other industrialized nations as Great Britain, France, Germany, and Italy. In Germany, because of the depression and war reparations from World War I, inflation skyrocketed, and German money became almost worthless. This combination of national humiliation and poverty led directly to the rise of Adolf Hitler to power in the 1930's.

Hoover was justifiably criticized for his reaction to the Bonus Boys camping out in the Washington D.C. area in the summer of 1932. The Bonus Boys were World War I veterans who had been promised a bonus for their service to their country in World War I. These World War I veterans were not supposed to get their bonus till 1945, but because the Great Depression was so bad, they wanted their bonuses early.

President Hoover ordered these World War I veterans out of the area; General Douglas MacArthur commanded the troops who cleared the veterans out. There may have been as many as 20,000 veterans in this shanty town in Washington D.C. at approximately 4:30 P.M. on July 28, 1932, when the U.S. military not only pushed these men out of the area, they also burned down their shanty town.

Hoover's attack on the Bonus marchers and the beginning of the Great Depression cost him the upcoming presidential election against Franklin Delano Roosevelt in November 1932. Not surprisingly, FDR won a landslide victory.

Herbert Hoover 31st President (March 4, 1929 to March 4, 1933)
http://cdn.loc.gov/service/pnp/cph/3a00000/3a02000/3a02000/3a02089r.jpg

The 32nd President: Franklin Delano Roosevelt

Franklin Delano Roosevelt was the 32nd President of the United States (March 4, 1933-April 12, 1945).

Born: January 30, 1882

Hyde Park, New York

Died: April 12, 1945 (aged 63)

Warm Springs, Georgia

Education: Attended Groton High School in Massachusetts. Attended Harvard from 1900 to 1903 and graduated in 1903 with an undergraduate degree. (Officially class of 1904). He attended Columbia Law School between 1905 and 1907 but never graduated.

Political Party Affiliation: Democrat

Family: Franklin Roosevelt married his cousin, Eleanor Roosevelt; they had four children. (President Roosevelt will be referred to hereafter as FDR). He also struggled after contracting polio in 1921 and was virtually crippled, though he learned to walk with braces and considered it important to be seen as leading while on his feet.

FDR's Office and Domestic Agenda:

Franklin Delano Roosevelt was the longest-serving president in our history. He was elected to four terms (though he died early in his 4th term). Before becoming president, FDR had also served as a New York State Senator, and like his cousin, Theodore Roosevelt, had also been Assistant Secretary of the Navy and Governor of New York. During FDR's first (busy) one hundred days in office, the U.S.

Congress passed the Social Security Act, which promised to give senior citizens a monthly stipend,

based on their lifetime earnings, to live on for the remainder of their lives, or as long as they qualified

for it. This was important relief for older people, most of whom could no longer work long hard hours

but still needed to buy groceries and pay their home expenses.

A New Gold Policy

On June 5, 1933, the United States went off the gold standard, a monetary system in which paper

money is backed by gold, which had been U.S. policy since 1879. Congress nullified creditors' rights to

have his or her money exchanged for gold, because when banks began to fail after the stock market

crash, many Americans started hiding their money in their homes. FDR believed if Americans hoarded

gold too, the U.S. would no longer be able to back gold with their money. FDR declared a banking

holiday and ordered banks not to pay debts in gold or to export gold, either.

FDR believed in Keynesian Economics, named after British economist John Maynard Keynes (June

5, 1883-April 21, 1946). One part of Keynesian economics is that in a downturn of an economy, a

country must inflate its money supply. Britain had gone off the gold standard in 1931. FDR signed

Executive Order #6102, which ordered all Americans, except jewelers, dentists and other merchants

who dealt specifically with gold, to turn in all their gold in denominations greater than $100, gold

coins, gold bullion, and gold certificates to the Federal Reserve. Americans had until May 1, 1933, to

turn in their gold; if they did not, they would be committing a felony; if convicted, they could spend up

to ten years in jail, with an additional fine of $10,000 (in 1933 dollars!)

FDR announced this policy on April 5, 1933, giving Americans less than a month to turn in their gold tender. By May 10, the Federal Reserve had taken in $300 billion in gold, with citizens receiving

$20.67 per ounce in exchange.

Once the Federal Reserve had accumulated all the gold it believed was coming it, it raised the price of gold per ounce to $35.00 (inflating the price 69%). The price of gold would stay at $35/ounce until August 15, 1971, when President Richard Nixon took the U.S. off the gold standard. On December 31, 1974, President Gerald Ford signed legislation that made it legal for Americans to own gold bullion again in $100.00 or more.

FDR's Foreign Policy

After promising for years to keep America out of the war brewing with Germany, FDR asked Congress to declare war on Japan after the Japanese attacked Pearl Harbor on December 7, 1941, decimating the United States Navy, sinking battleships like the *U.S.S. Arizona* and the *U.S.S. Oklahoma*. While there were no aircraft carriers at Pearl Harbor at the time of the attack, Japanese forces also destroyed airplanes, dockyards, and airfields, and killed over 3,000 American sailors. Because Japan had a treaty with Germany and Italy (as Axis powers), once the U.S. declared war on Japan, Germany and Italy declared war on us as well. This led to a two-front war, where we fought both in Europe and in the Pacific.

World War II

Major Battles of the European Campaign

While the U.S., woefully unprepared for war, developed a crash program to train, equip and move

men and arms to Europe and the Pacific, Germany marched through Europe, conquering country after

country, while Japan concentrated its military might on dominating the Pacific theater. At one point,

Germany controlled Austria, Poland, France, Belgium, the Netherlands, Denmark, Hungary and parts

of North Africa.

After two and a half years of battle in Europe, General Dwight D. Eisenhower invaded France with a

combined Allied army of thousands on the beaches of Normandy, on June 6, 1944 (D-Day). The U.S.,

Great Britain, and other Allies were eventually able to drive a wedge in the Nazi military forces

occupying France. But the cost in lives was enormous; ten thousand men died on that first day of battle.

The second key battle was the Battle of the Bulge, in the Ardennes forest in Belgium. Half a million

German forces attacked the Allies and tried to split them apart by driving to Antwerp in northern

Belgium; by doing this, Hitler hoped to make a separate peace with the American and British forces. If

he could achieve that separate peace, Hitler intended to switch his forces to the East and attack the

Soviet forces threatening Berlin. The German forces eventually ran out of gas and manpower in this

month-long battle, from December 16, 1944 to January 16, 1945. In the final significant battle, the

Soviet Union attacked Germany's capital, Berlin, in the latter part of April 1945 and by May 2, the

Soviet Union had overrun and conquered the city, although there would be no peace treaty between the

Allies and the German leaders until May 9, 1945.

Major Battles of the Pacific Campaign

The turning point of the naval struggle was the Battle of Midway in 1942, in which the U.S. Navy was able to block Japanese expansion to Australia. Other victories included the Battle of Guadalcanal

in 1944 and the Battle of Leyte Gulf in 1945, which allowed U.S. military forces to return to the

Philippines. The U.S. military forces captured the island of Iwo Jima in 1945; this was important

strategically, because if the U.S. had ended up invading Japan, Iwo Jima would have served as a launch

pad for the Army and Navy Air Forces to strike the Japanese homeland. When the U.S. plane the *Enola*

Gay dropped the atomic bomb on Hiroshima on August 6, 1945 and a second on Nagasaki on August 9,

1945, Japan did finally surrender; the surrender took place on September 2, 1945, aboard *the U.S.S.*

Missouri.

Presidential Firsts for FDR

FDR is the only president ever elected to office four times and he died on April 12, 1945 while

serving his fourth term. With the passing of the 22nd Constitutional amendment, presidential terms of

office were limited to two. Two constitutional amendments were passed while F.D.R. was in office. The

20th Amendment changed the inaugural date of incoming presidents from March 4th, to January 20th,

which forever changed the transition period of incoming presidents. This was passed on January 23,

1933; FDR's second inauguration took place on January 20, 1937.

The 21st Amendment repealed Prohibition and made it legal to make and sell alcohol in the U.S.

again. The 21st amendment was ratified on December 3, 1933. FDR struggled with polio throughout his

presidency. On April 12, 1945, he suffered a massive cerebral hemorrhage while at his vacation home

in Warm Springs, Georgia, and died. He did not live to see the triumphant end of the war he had led

America into.

Franklin Delano Roosevelt 32nd President (March 4, 1933 to April 12, 1945)
htttp://www.history.com/topics/us-presidents/franklin delano
roosevelt/pictures/franklin delano roosevelt

The 33rd President: Harry S Truman

Harry Truman was the 33rd President of the United States (April 12, 1945-January 20, 1953).

Born: May 8, 1884

Lamar, Missouri

Died: December 26, 1972 (aged 88)

Kansas, Missouri

Education: Spalding's Commercial College; University of Missouri-Kansas School of Law; he did not graduate.

Political Party Affiliation: Democrat

Harry Truman's Domestic Policy

Harry Truman continued the policies of his predecessor Franklin Roosevelt with the Fair Deal. This would see the federal government take a more active role in American society. For instance, Truman signed an executive order that ended segregation in the military in 1948, but this would not really affect military units until 1950, with the start of the Korean War. Truman dealt with a number of strikes in industry and created a number of emergency decrees that allowed him to take various actions to deal with these strikes. Truman also had to deal with all the soldiers coming home after World War II and being assimilated back into U.S. society. By one estimate, as many as fifteen million men were in uniform by the end of World War II.

One program paid returning veterans $50 a week for fifty-two weeks. The G.I. Bill also allowed returning veterans the opportunity to go to college; many could never have afforded to go otherwise.

The 1948 Presidential Election

The 1948 Presidential Election was one of the most contentious in U.S. election history. The Democratic Party split into three groups: Strom Thurmond broke off and formed the Dixiecrats, a group composed of pro-segregation white southerners; his former Secretary of State Henry Wallace wanted to work with the Soviet Union, and the third group was made up of Harry Truman and the remaining members of the Democratic Party.   Thomas A. Dewey, running on the Republican ticket, did not even campaign that hard. He made only a few political speeches, thinking he was a shoo-in to win over Truman, while Truman campaigned hard, going by train from town to town and making speeches standing on the caboose. *The Chicago Tribune* printed a paper on Election Night, claiming Dewey had won the election, but when the returns came in the *Tribune* had to retract their story. Truman won 303 electoral votes; Thomas Dewey won 189 electoral votes. Strom Thurmond won 39 electoral votes. Henry Wallace didn't win any. In fact, many scholars believe that it was the black vote in many cities nationwide that allowed Truman to win, because he had desegregated the U.S. military.

President Truman's Foreign Policy

When Harry Truman became president on April 12, 1945 with the death of FDR, he had important decisions to make. The war was ending in Europe, but Japan was stubbornly refusing to surrender. If the U.S. tried to attack Japan on the ground, experts were predicting there could be a million casualties.

It was Truman's decision to drop the atomic bombs on Japan, ending World War II. To this day, he is the only president ever to have used a nuclear weapon.

He also decided to have the U.S. join the United Nations, the successor to the League of Nations.

The United Nations is an international organization created to give nations around the world an alternative to war by letting them resolve their differences peacefully, through diplomacy.

FDR's widow, Eleanor Roosevelt, helped to build this international legislative body.

The Truman Doctrine

President Truman went to a joint session of Congress on January 27, 1947, and asked Congress for $400 million to fight communism subversion, whether internally or externally. The two countries that many historians say that Truman was thinking of was Greece and Turkey. Greece was facing an internal rebellion, and the country was facing a possible invasion by the Soviet Union or Soviet allies.

President Trump supported the domino theory, that if the U.S. stood by and let these countries fall then communists around the country would be encouraged to start other revolutions and countries would fall like dominoes around the world. This theory would be adopted by future presidents such as Dwight Eisenhower.

The Cold War (the title given by scholars to the struggles between the Soviet Union and America between 1948 and 1989) began just after World War II, between President Truman and then-Soviet leader Joseph Stalin. Berlin, the conquered capital of Germany, had been divided up into four zones, each run by a different ally (the U.S., France, Great Britain and the Soviet Union). However, bent on conquering Berlin and turning it communist, Soviet forces began blockading Berlin in 1948 and 1949 (approximate dates are June 24, 1948 to May 12, 1949). The U.S. Air Force, together with the British Air Force, for almost one year, flew planes of food, water, coal and medicine, around the clock, in all kinds of weather, into Berlin to ensure that Berliners did not starve or surrender to the Soviets. This courageous act was The Berlin Airlift.

In 1948, President Truman recognized Israel as an independent Jewish state in the Middle East. In 1949, the North Atlantic Treaty Organization (NATO) was formed to show U.S. support in case the Soviets invaded Europe through Berlin. Harry Truman also sent United Nation troops into South Korea in 1950 to protect them from the expansionist policies of communist North Korea. This war lasted until 1953.

The Korean War (1950-1953)

After World War II, Korea was a colony controlled by Japan. When Japan was defeated, both the U.S. and the Soviet Union divided the Korean peninsula at the 38th parallel. In the northern part of the peninsula, with its capital at Pyongyang, the Soviets created a communist government. In the southern part of the peninsula, with its capital at Seoul, the Americans created a capitalist government. Both the north and the south wanted the Korean peninsula united under their form of government.

On June 25, 1950, the North Koreans attacked South Korea with an army of approximately 135,000 men and quickly overran Seoul. President Truman responded on June 27, 1950, declaring that this was a police action; he ordered U.S. troops to help the fleeing soldiers of the Republic of Korea (ROK). However, it was not until September 1950 that the Supreme Commander of U.N. Forces, Douglas MacArthur, launched his brilliant amphibious result at Inchon, Seoul's port city, and outflanked North Korea's army; the North Koreans retreated to North Korea.

The U.N. troops took back all the territory that they had lost to the North Koreans a year later MacArthur then decreed that the U.N. forces would destroy the communist regime of North Korea. China's leader Mao Zedong warned both the U.S. and the U.N. that if U.N. forces invaded China's territory, China would join the war. Mao Zedong kept his word: on November 26, 1950, a Chinese army attacked and pushed back the U.N. army, forcing the U.N. army to retreat down to South Korea and Seoul. On January 21, 1951, that U.N. forces began using their superior fire power (air power, heavy artillery, and lighter artillery such as mortars) to balance China's superior manpower. By March 14, 1951, U.N. forces retook Seoul. For the next couple of years, until the armistice was signed on July 27, 1953, the Korean War was a limited war, or stalemate, with many casualties on both sides.

The Significance of the Korean War

On the political side, President Truman fired General MacArthur on April 11, 1951, because General MacArthur had publicly criticized Truman's war strategy. This was a very unpopular move; MacArthur was well liked by most of the American public. American casualties alone were almost 37,000 killed. With troops wounded and missing, the toll for the U.S. alone rises to 169,365.

South Korea had 984,000 total casualties while both North Korea and China had over 900,000 each, and these are just the military casualties. The civilian casualties may never be known for both North and South Korea. North and South Korea are still divided today along the 38th parallel. The two Koreas have never signed a peace treaty (an armistice was signed on July 27, 1953, but not a formal peace treaty). One could argue that the Korean peninsula is still at war. Today, tensions between capitalistic South Korea and communist, repressive North Korea are still high. Afterward, many U.S. presidents chose to follow Truman's example of fighting limited wars: The Vietnam War (1965-1973); The Persian Gulf War (1990-1991) and the Iraq War (2003-present) and Afghanistan (2001-present) in which the U.S. is involved in endless wars with no real exit strategy and enormous costs in lives and money.

111

Harry Truman 33rd President (April 12, 1945 to January 20, 1953)
http://cdn.loc.gov/service/pnp/cph/3a50000/3a55000/3a55000/3a55064v.jpg

The 34th President: Dwight D. Eisenhower

Dwight D. Eisenhower was the 34th President of the United States (January 20, 1953-January 20, 1961).

Born: October 14, 1890

Denison, Texas

Died: March 29, 1969 (aged 78)

Washington, D.C.

Education: U.S. Military Academy (West Point) Graduates class of 1915

Political Party Affiliation: Republican

Eisenhower's Domestic Policy

Eisenhower signed the Federal Aid Highway Act in 1956, creating the interstate system crisscrossing America, making travel by automobile much easier and safer, and helping to facilitate trade, tourism and communication. The 1940s and 1950s was a time of great expansion of America's suburbs. This was also the beginning of the generation known as Baby Boomers (1946-1964) in which the U.S population was growing substantially. In 1957, Eisenhower signed a civil-rights bill, but Congress amended the final bill, making it much weaker than Eisenhower had intended.

He intervened when then-Arkansas governor Orval Fabus ordered National Guard troops to block nine black children from entering a predominantly white school, preventing desegregation, which by then was the law of the land, through the landmark court decision Brown vs. Board of Education

(1954), which Eisenhower did not speak about publicly, officially keeping a neutral stance.

Privately, he was afraid of violence because of desegregation. So Eisenhower ordered army soldiers

to make sure that there was no trouble at the school, and the nine black children entered peacefully.

In 1955, Eisenhower suffered a heart attack while on vacation in Denver. For the rest of his

Administration, his health was a great concern.

Eisenhower's Foreign Policy

Korea was a major headache for Eisenhower, and at one point he threatened to use nuclear weapons

to end the standoff. Many people believed him. The threat eventually led to the Americans, North and

South Koreans, and Chinese signing an armistice, ending the conflict on July 27, 1953. President

Eisenhower's ending the Korean War is a significant part of his legacy. Under his presidency, the

Central Intelligence Agency (CIA) sponsored the overthrow of governments in Iran and Guatemala; he

also sent U.S. troops into Lebanon in 1958 to stem some of the fighting occurring in that area.

Soviet Aggression in Eastern Europe

The Soviets put down a rebellion in East Germany in Berlin on June 16-June 17, 1953, after the

death of Stalin. The Soviet Union had been taking huge amounts of East Germany's produced goods

from 1945 to 1953. When Stalin died, many East Berliners were upset; they rioted until Soviet police

and military forces went into these areas and suppressed the rioters. In 1955, the Soviet leadership

created the Warsaw Pact, a military alliance of Eastern bloc countries (Poland and East Germany, to

name a few) joined together to counter the Western military alliance of NATO.

Political Agitation in Poland, Hungary, and Cuba

In 1956, the Polish leader Wladyslaw Gomulka began talking publicly about re-evaluating Poland's relationship with the Soviet Union. The Polish military showed enormous courage, actually sending their tanks to confront Soviet troops. The Soviet Union backed down. Then-Soviet leader Nikita Khrushchev and Gomulka were able to work out a deal, and the two countries did not go to war.

However, Hungarian leader Imre Nagy started talking about leaving the Warsaw Pact, and leaving the Soviet Union altogether, and the Soviet leaders would not allow that. In 1956, Khrushchev ordered Soviet military forces to invade Budapest, the capital of Hungary, and the surrounding areas, and these forces crushed the Hungarian uprising, with thousands of Hungarians dying. In 1957, the Soviet Union surprised the U.S. and the world when they launched *Sputnik*, the world's first satellite, into space. This immediately put them ahead in the budding space race, with America falling behind and eventually beginning a crash program to identify and train astronauts and build crafts which could take them into space and return them safely to earth.

In 1959, Fidel Castro seized power in Cuba from Fulgencio Batista, and eventually became a Western-hemisphere ally of the Soviet Union. The 1950s and early 1960s was a time of high tensions between the Soviet Union and the United States; it looked like there could be nuclear war between the two superpowers. However, when Eisenhower left office on January 20, 1961, the U.S. and the Soviet Union were at peace. This is an important part of Eisenhower's legacy.

115

Dwight Eisenhower 34th President (January 20, 1953 to January 20, 1961)
http://cdn.loc.gov/service/pnp/cph/3c00000/3c04000/3c04600/3c04631v.jpg

The 35th President: John F. Kennedy

John Fitzgerald Kennedy was the 35th President of the United States (January 20, 1961-November 22, 1963).

Born: May 29, 1917

Brookline, Massachusetts

Died: November 22, 1963 (aged 46)

Dallas, Texas

Education: Harvard University: Bachelor's degree. Additional schooling at Stanford University and the London School of Economics.

Political Party Affiliation: Democrat

(The 23rd Constitutional Amendment took effect on March 29, 1961. This amendment gives Washington D.C. three electoral votes, even though Washington D.C. is the capitol of the U.S., not a state).

John Fitzgerald Kennedy, a World War II hero for his actions in the Pacific theater with PT-109, was the youngest man ever elected to the presidency (he was 43), and one of the wealthiest: his father,

Joseph P. Kennedy was a self-made multi-millionaire who had served as the first chairman of the Security & Exchange Commission under FDR and later served as the Ambassador to the Court of St. James. Jack, the second of nine Kennedy children, had been a U.S. Congressman and a United States Senator before running for president against Richard Nixon, Eisenhower's vice-president. In one of the closest presidential elections of all time, Kennedy finally won when he won the state of Illinois in the early-morning hours after Election Day.

When Kennedy took office on January 20, 1961, with his "New Frontier" programs, the U.S. was already in a Cold War with the Soviet Union and Kennedy was aware of the dangers. In his 1961 inaugural address, he made the following famous statement: "Ask not what your country can do for you; ask what you can do for your country".

Kennedy's Domestic Policy

Civil rights for black Americans was a leading concern during Kennedy's presidency, especially with the issue of ongoing segregation in the American South. The Supreme Court had already begun the dismantling of segregation with its landmark case, *Brown vs. the Board of Education* (1954), which declared that segregation was unconstitutional. Eisenhower continued that progress with the desegregation of schools like Central High School in Little Rock, Arkansas. President Kennedy was also aware of civil-rights leader, Dr. Martin Luther King. When he heard that King had been arrested in Birmingham, Alabama, President Kennedy made a point to call him while in jail to show his support for the civil rights movement.

Kennedy's Foreign Policy

President Kennedy inherited the plans for a CIA-sponsored invasion of Cuba from the Eisenhower Administration; this invasion occurred at the Bay of Pigs from April 17-April 19, 1961, just after his term had begun. This invasion turned out to be a military debacle, in which the 1400 trained Cuban exiles were quickly surrounded, arrested and imprisoned. President Kennedy refused to provide air support for the invading Cubans because with the Soviet Union backing Cuba, he did not want to take the chance of triggering World War III. Later, he said that the CIA had lied to him about the scope of

the invasion and that they wanted him to authorize air support to trigger that war he was afraid to start. President Kennedy came out on television and took responsibility for the catastrophe. "Why is it that victory has a hundred fathers while defeat is an orphan?" The Bay of Pigs made Kennedy look weak and indecisive.

After the Bay of Pigs, the Cuban leader, Fidel Castro, sought a closer alliance with the Soviet Union, which eventually led, in 1962, to the Soviet Union putting nuclear missiles in Cuba and the Cuban Missile Crisis (October 16-October 28, 1962). This thirteen-day showdown between the U.S. and the Soviet Union almost led to World War III and a nuclear confrontation. It was the closest the U.S. ever came to the use of nuclear weapons, after the bombings of Hiroshima and Nagasaki which ended World War II.

President Kennedy ordered a blockade of Cuba, and the U.S. Navy forced the Soviet Navy, which was bringing supplies to Cuba, to turn around and go back to the Soviet Union. The U.S. and the Soviets finally resolved their differences by agreeing that the U.S. would give up its missiles in Turkey, which were aimed at the Soviet Union and that the Soviet Union would immediately dismantle their missiles on Cuba. Afterward, a red phone (essentially an emergency phone) was installed in the White

House with a direct link to Moscow, to prevent nuclear war from happening simply through a misunderstanding.

Kennedy also inspired the U.S. to boost its NASA space program and aspire to land a man on the moon by the end of the decade (a man would land on the moon on July 20, 1969). The Kennedy White House was glamorous, under the influence of Jackie Kennedy, America's most glamorous First Lady, who brought artists, musicians and writers to Washington and restored the White House through a special construction project. When it was finished, she starred in a national television program to re-introduce Americans to the First Residence. Their two children, Caroline and John Jr., were very popular with Americans as well.

In November 1963, the Kennedys traveled to Texas for a three-day political trip. On November 22nd, while riding in a motorcade through Dallas, Kennedy was shot and killed. Lee Harvey Oswald, the 24-year-old former Marine who had defected to the Soviet Union, was arrested and charged with the crime. Two days after the president died, Oswald was himself shot by Dallas nightclub owner Jack Ruby in the basement of the Dallas Police Department, as he was being transferred to the county jail. He died at Parkland Hospital, where JFK had died, an hour later.

After Kennedy's death, Jackie Kennedy was worried that his presidency would be forgotten. She summoned Theodore White, a journalist, to meet her at the Kennedy family compound in Hyannis port, Massachusetts a week after the assassination and told him that Kennedy's presidency had been an American version of Camelot. To this day, people think of Kennedy's presidency as a glorious moment in American history.

John Fitzgerald Kennedy 35th President (January 20, 1961 to November 22, 1963)
http://cdn.loc.gov/service/pnp/cph/3a50000/3a53000/3a53300/3a53304r.jpg

The 36th President: Lyndon Baines Johnson

Lyndon Baines Johnson was the 36th President of the United States (November 22, 1963-January 20, 1969.)

Born: August 27, 1908

Gillespie County, Texas

Died: January 22, 1973 (aged 64)

San Antonio, Texas

Education: Texas State University: Bachelor's degree.

Political Party Affiliation: Democrat

When John F. Kennedy was shot and killed in Dallas, Texas, his vice-president, Lyndon Johnson, became the 36th president. Johnson completed Kennedy's term and was then elected, in a landslide victory in 1964, to his own term. Before serving as Kennedy's vice-president, Johnson was a Texas school teacher and later, a Congressman from Texas and a powerful Senator. One of his first acts was to form The Warren Commission, headed by Supreme Court Chief Justice Earl Warren, to investigate the assassination of Kennedy and present their findings to him. The Commission worked for a year and presented Johnson with the Warren Commission Report in September 1964, which stated that Lee Harvey Oswald alone had killed Kennedy. They also presented 26 volumes of evidence to back up their claims.

Johnson's Domestic Policy

Johnson's presidency had several major pieces of legislation; the two most memorable are the Civil

Rights Act of 1964 and the Voting Rights Act of 1965.

The Civil Rights Act of 1964 was signed into law by President Johnson on July 2, 1964. This law

ended segregation in the South, but also in other parts of the country. This allowed blacks the same

privileges in public places, like bathrooms, restaurants, and movie theaters, that whites already enjoyed.

The Voting Rights Act of 1965 guaranteed that black voters could not be intimidated into not voting in

local and national elections. In fact, during Johnson's Presidency, the 24th Constitutional Amendment,

outlawing poll taxes, was passed (January 23, 1964).

Poll taxes were a device used by election officials at the polls to prevent blacks from voting; they

were told they had to pay a certain amount of money to cast a vote, usually a $1.00 or more. Many

black voters were poor, poll taxes meant that black voters would not cast ballots. The 24th Amendment

made it illegal for any voter to be charged a poll tax while voting in federal elections.

The Voting Rights Act was signed into law on August 6, 1965. This law outlawed other practices

that Southern states had used since the U.S. Civil War and Reconstruction to prevent blacks from

voting. This included a literacy test; if a potential black voter wanted to vote, he or she had to read a

passage either from the U.S. Constitution or the state constitution. Election officials administered the

tests; if they did not like the voter's responses, the election official failed the voter on the spot. In this

way black voters—even medical doctors and lawyers—were prevented from voting. The Voting

Rights Act ended all these arbitrary 'tests' once and for all.

President Johnson also instituted his "Great Society" programs, which included Medicare and

Medicaid. These were signed into law by President Johnson on July 30, 1965.

Medicare was enacted to help people 65 years old or older who often did not have health insurance for stays in the hospitals. Medicaid was created to help the poor in American society who often could not afford extended hospital stays or other health costs.

The stated goals of Johnson's Great Society and the War on Poverty were the elimination of poverty and racial injustice. Initially, his programs enjoyed some success; between 1963 and 1970 poor people made up 22.2 percent of American society, and by 1970, the American poor had dropped to 12.6 percent. Other goals of his program were clean air and water, more educational opportunities, and trying to make Americans healthier by lessening disease. However, Johnson's Great Society required a great deal of government spending. During Johnson's administration the Vietnam War was heating up, with more and more U.S. troops being sent there. Increased spending on the Vietnam War meant less spending on the Great Society.

Johnson's Foreign Policy

President Johnson was the president who expanded the role of U.S. military forces in Vietnam, from military advisors under Kennedy to a fighting force under Johnson. By 1968, 500,000 men were fighting in Southeast Asia. The stated purpose was to prevent the spread of communism, thus preventing communist North Vietnam from taking over its neighbor, South Vietnam, which was democratic. The enemy included not only the North Vietnamese Army, but also the Vietcong—guerrilla fighters from the South who were fighting on the North Vietnamese side.

Instead of conventional warfare, the terrain of Vietnam demanded the use of guerrilla tactics and jungle fighting, which U.S. forces were not trained or experienced in. The war dragged on for years,

with Americans winning every major battle, but back home, returning soldiers and young liberals on college campuses were angry. They began to protest the war, getting louder and more militant each time. So while America was winning in Vietnam, she was losing the public relations battle at home. There was little appetite for fighting a war in a country no one cared about, trying to prevent the spread of communism thousands of miles away.

With hundreds of thousands of protesting Americans rioting in the streets and a war stuck in a stalemate in Vietnam, Johnson announced he would neither seek nor accept his party's nomination for the presidency in 1968, opening the door to other Democratic candidates.

Robert Francis Kennedy (November 20, 1925 to June 6, 1968), JFK's brother, decided to run, and entered the race late. He won the crucial primary election in California, but as he was thanking campaign workers afterward, in the kitchen of the Ambassador Hotel in Los Angeles, he was shot by a Palestinian terrorist Sir Han Sir Han on June 5, 1968 and died the next day.

Civil-rights leader Martin Luther King was killed eight weeks earlier, in Memphis, Tennessee.

Johnson retired to his Texas ranch and died of a heart attack in early 1973.

Lyndon Baines Johnson 36th President of the United States (November 22,1963-
        January 20, 1969) htttp://www.history.com/topics/us-presidents/lyndon-b-
        johnson/pictures

The 37th President: Richard Nixon

Richard Milhous Nixon was the 37th president of the United States (January 20, 1969-August 9, 1974).

Born: January 9, 1913

Yorba Linda, California

Died: April 22, 1994 (aged 81)

Manhattan, New York

Education: Whittier College: Bachelor's degree; Dukc University School of Law: Bachelor of Laws

Political Party Affiliation: Republican

Nixon's presidency marked a watershed for the American public. He was the only president to date who has ever resigned the office, amid the chaos of Watergate, the greatest political scandal of its time. After Americans learned of the crimes of his Administration, the overwhelming belief we had had in our Chief Executive evaporated. To this day, our skepticism about politicians is rooted in the sense of betrayal Americans felt over the revelations of Watergate. The 26th constitutional amendment, lowering the voting age from 21 to 18, was ratified by both houses of Congress and three-quarters of the U.S. States (38) by July 1, 1971; President Nixon signed it into law on July 5, 1971. This allowed more people to vote in more elections.

Nixon's Domestic Policy

President Richard Nixon came into office saying he would govern with the consent of the silent majority and restore law and order again in American society. Born to a poor family in California, he earned his law degree there, joined the Navy in 1942 and began his career in Congress in 1946, eventually becoming Eisenhower's vice-president for eight years. He failed to win the presidency in 1960 and then lost when he ran for governor of California. After that, he said he was retiring from politics, but in 1968 he made a dramatic comeback and won the White House.

Nixon created the Environmental Protection Agency (EPA) in 1970, a new government agency with broad sweeping powers to pass and enforce regulations to stop individuals and corporations from polluting the environment. Most of all, it was concerned with cleaning out the pollution in our air and water. As part of his campaign promise to end the war in Vietnam, Nixon launched a secret bombing campaign in Cambodia, from April 29-July 22, 1970, which U.S. and South Vietnamese military forces had taken part in, to destroy the North Vietnamese military supply lines. Nixon had promised to end the war and now to many college students it appeared that Nixon was widening the war. College campus protests grew larger and more disorderly. At Kent State University in Ohio, four students were killed by the National Guard during a campus protest in May 1970. This only made the outcry louder.

Nixon took the U.S. dollar off the gold standard and set it to a floating currency, on August 15, 1971. Now world currency rates would dictate the purchasing power of the dollar, not the U.S. dollar's relationship to actual gold. The same day, Nixon also instituted a series of wage and price controls. Though his price and wage control actions lasted for only 90 days, Nixon also said that he would create a pay board and price commissions. (However, public response to his wage and price controls was so negative, he never created the pay board and price commission.) Scholars have labeled the two actions that the president took as "Nixon Shock".

Nixon's Proposal for a Health Care Plan for All Americans

Nixon tried both in 1971, and again in 1974, with a new program called Comprehensive Health Insurance Program (CHIP for short), to give all Americans a basic health-insurance plan for short- or long-term stays in the hospital. He outlined his ideas in a proposal that he sent to Congress on February 6, 1974. Congress was divided on the proposal: conservatives said it went too far and liberals claimed it did not go far enough. By mid-1974, Nixon was so involved with the Watergate scandal that he did not try harder to implement CHIP.

Nixon's Foreign Policy: "Only Nixon could go to China"

President Nixon built his political career on exposing communists, including Alger Hiss, a high-ranking member of FDR's staff during the 1930s. Eyewitness testimony later revealed that Hiss was a Soviet spy, who had been passing along classified secrets to the Soviets in the 1930s.

Hiss perjured himself in an espionage trial. When the perjury was discovered later, Hiss went to jail for five years. Nixon's pursuit of Hiss unleashed a firestorm of controversy between the left and the right wing political parties in America. However, Nixon did not back down and won the perjury conviction.

In 1972, when Nixon wanted to establish trade and diplomatic relations with China, he was the one president who could do so without being labeled a communist. Nixon met with Chinese leader Mao Zedong, and diplomatic and commercial relations were established.

Detente

President Nixon wanted a peaceful mutual coexistence with the Soviet Union. There may not always be total peace, but there would not be war, either. When in 1969 there was a border war between China and the Soviet Union on the borders of Mongolia, and it seemed that this border war could lead to an actual hot war between the Soviet Union and China, Nixon let the Soviets know that in the event of war, he would support China. (This later became known as the "China" card).

However, eventually tensions between the two countries became peaceful. Nixon met with Soviet leader Leonid Brezhnev and worked out the Strategic Arms Limitations Treaty or SALT in 1972, limiting the number of nuclear missiles that could be manufactured annually. What emerged in Nixon's foreign policy was a triangular effect: with the U.S. working with both China and the Soviet Union (the two military allies of North Vietnam), this would force North Vietnam to the bargaining table to work out a peace treaty, so that the U.S. could withdraw from Vietnam.

 The Nixon policy was to withdraw American troops over time, so the South Vietnamese government would not collapse all at once. This was called Vietnamization of the war. South Vietnamese troops would be trained by American forces and would be able to defend themselves. Over time, Nixon reduced the number of U.S. troops in Vietnam went from 500,000 in 1969 to 24,000 U.S. troops by 1972.

The U.S. Air Force remained a powerful asset; it was primarily through bombings that the Easter Offensive launched by the North Vietnamese conventional forces in 1972 was stopped. This invading army had approximately 120,000 men, and the air power of the U.S. may have killed as many as 40,000 to 75,000 KIA, with 60,000 wounded. These air attacks helped stop the NVA army in its tracks.

The U.S. and South Vietnamese forces suffered 10,000 killed, 33,000 wounded and 3,500 missing.

The battle occurred between March 30-October 22, 1972.

While the leadership of Hanoi was arguing about the shape of the table in Paris where they were supposed to hammer out a peace treaty, Nixon bombed Hanoi, the capital of North Vietnam; shortly afterward, the North Vietnamese went back to negotiations, and the U.S., North Vietnam, and South Vietnam signed a peace treaty in Paris on January 23, 1973. Nixon announced the end of the war on national television, describing the U.S. pull-out of its military forces in Vietnam as 'peace with honor'. Officially, the last U.S. soldier left of Vietnam on March 29, 1973, though many listed as missing in action were still in North Vietnamese prison camps. On April 30, 1975, Saigon fell to North Vietnamese forces and Vietnam was militarily reunited under a communist regime.

Watergate

Watergate was the political scandal that defined Nixon's presidency. Whatever else he accomplished that was positive has been overlooked in light of the crimes his men committed on his behalf.
On June 17, 1972, five men were arrested at the Democratic National Headquarters at the Watergate Hotel in Washington D.C. These men had been ordered by their immediate boss, G. Gordon Liddy, to break in and discover whatever incriminating evidence or intelligence that they could discover on the Democrats by setting wiretaps or photographing documents. It was an election year and the President's men were looking for any advantage they could get in the upcoming presidential election.

Though Nixon easily won reelection over the Democratic candidate George McGovern that November, two young investigative reporters for the *Washington Post,* Bob Woodward and Carl Bernstein, began to report exclusively on the story. Soon it became apparent that this was not a random one-time break-in, that the President's men were engaged in many dirty tricks to derail McGovern's campaign, and before that, the campaigns of other Democratic presidential candidates who had more potential to beat Nixon. Bob Woodward had an important deep-background source he met in dimly-lit garages, whom he nicknamed Deep Throat. Deep Throat fed Woodward a lot of information which eventually led all the way to President Nixon.

The question became, "What did the president know, and when did he know it?"

The U.S. Congress created a committee to investigate Nixon's activities. When they discovered that Nixon had secretly been tape-recording his conversations with all the people in the Oval Office, Congress demanded these tapes. Nixon refused and tried to claim claimed executive privilege. Congress went to the Supreme Court; the Supreme Court in its decision stated that Nixon could not claim executive privilege in this matter; he needed to turn over the tapes. When the Congressional committee became to write up articles of impeachment one for obstruction of justice, it was clear Nixon needed to resign, which he did on August 9, 1974.

Gerald R. Ford, who became Nixon's vice-president when his original vice-president, Spiro Agnew, resigned over his own corruption scandal, became the 38th president. He is the only president ever to reach the presidency without having been elected to either office first.

Richard Milhouse Nixon 37th President of the United States (January 20, 1969-
August 9, 1974) htttp://www.history.com/topics/us-presidents/richard-m-nixon/

The 38th President: Gerald R. Ford

Gerald Ford was the 38th President of the United States (August 9, 1974-January 20, 1977).

Born: July 14, 1913

Omaha, Nebraska

Died: December 26, 2006 (aged 93)

Rancho Mirage, California

Education: University of Michigan: Bachelor's degree; Yale Law School: Bachelor of Laws;

Political Party Affiliation: Republican

Gerald Ford became Vice-President first in October 1973, when then-Vice-President Spiro Agnew was forced to resign because of bribery and tax evasion in office. although Ford was not confirmed by Congress until December 6, 1973. When Nixon was forced to resign because of Watergate in August 1974, Ford became president. Almost his first act as president was to sign a 'full and unconditional pardon' to Nixon, which saved Nixon from being tried, convicted and sent to jail for the Watergate crimes. This was the only time that the 25th amendment, passed in 1967, was invoked and approved by the U.S. Congress.

President Ford chose Nelson Rockefeller as his new vice-president.

President Ford did not get along well with the Democratic Congress. Ford was willing to help South Vietnam in its continuing fight with North Vietnam, but after years of war, Congress refused to aid

South Vietnam, and Saigon fell to North Vietnamese forces on April 30, 1975. Ford vetoed many pieces

of legislation from Congress while President, and did not choose his Vice-President Nelson Rockefeller

as his running mate in the 1976 presidential election; instead he chose a new running mate, Robert

Dole, because Rockefeller had declared he had no interest in being considered for Vice-President when

Ford ran for the presidential election in 1976. When Ford lost the 1976 election to Jimmy Carter, the

governor of Georgia, he decided to retire, saying that being president had been an unexpected bonus

after his long legislative career. (He had been a Congressman from Michigan since 1948).

Assassination Attempts

Lynette "Squeakie" Fromme was a member of the Charles Manson 'family', a group that terrorized

California by murdering actress Sharon Tate, her unborn child and several other people in the summer

of 1969. Fromme attempted to shoot Ford when he left the Capitol Rotunda of California in

Sacramento on September 5, 1975, as Ford was walking to meet the governor of California, Jerry

Brown. A Secret Service agent saw her before she could fire and wrestled her to the ground. Fromme's

gun had four bullets in it. President Ford kept his meeting with the governor and spoke to a breakfast

crowd at the Capitol. Ford did not mention the assassination attempt to Governor Jerry Brown until his

meeting was over.

On September 22, 1975, less than three weeks later, a deranged woman named Sara Jane Moore

fired at President Ford as he was getting into his car at approximately 3:30 P.M. at the San Francisco St.

Francis Hotel. The first shot barely missed him, and Secret Service agents were already pushing the

President into his armored limo when the second shot was fired. A nearby bystander Oliver Sipple

grabbed Moore's arm and deflected the second shot. This was the second time in less than three weeks

that a woman

tried to shoot President Ford while in California! Though President Ford had been an athlete in college, he was often clumsy in public. Comedian Chevy Chase became famous spoofing the president's falls and accidents on *Saturday Night Live*. The First Lady, Betty Ford, founded the Betty Ford Center for

substance abuse recovery in 1982, making drug and alcohol abuse less stigmatized than it had been before. Over the years, many people including celebrities have gotten clean and sober at the Betty Ford Center.

Ford left office on January 20, 1977.

Gerald Ford 38th President (August 9, 1974 to January 20,1977)
http://cdn.loc.gov/service/pnp/cph/3a50000/3a53000/3a53300/3a53307v.jpg

The 39th President: Jimmy Carter

Jimmy Carter was the 39th President of the United States (January 20, 1977-January 20, 1981).

Born: October 1, 1924 (Carter is 93)

Plains, Georgia

Education: U.S. Naval Academy: Graduated in class of 1946.

Political Party Affiliation: Democrat

President Jimmy Carter became president while the U.S. was going through a severe economic recession. Interest rates rocketed up to 21percent by the end of his Administration. Carter created the Department of Energy, with Arthur Schlesinger as its first Secretary. This newly created department dealt with the nuclear crisis on Three Mile Island in Pennsylvania in 1979, where it looked as though the nuclear core of the plant was going to melt but did not. This was a scary time in American history. Carter and his administration passed important legislation to put safeguards in place to prevent this from happening in the future. Meanwhile, there was a gas shortage all over the U.S. and in many places, gas was rationed, and fights broke out at gas pumps.

President Carter's Foreign Policy

Carter brought about a landmark peace treaty between Egypt and Israel and their leaders, Anwar Sadat and Menachem Begin, with the Camp David Accords, which were signed on September 17, 1978.

However, Carter's success with the Camp David Accords was erased with the Iran Hostage Crisis, which began in November 1979. The Ayatollah Khomeini seized power in Iran in December 1979, after the Shah fled the country and established a theocracy. The Ayatollah's followers seized the American

embassy in Tehran on November 4, 1979 and held the fifty-one workers there for four hundred and

forty-four days. The Carter State Department was helpless. These hostages were not be released until

Ronald Reagan took office on January 20, 1981.

President Carter's Accomplishments after he left the Presidency

Unlike most presidents, President Carter had a busy post-presidential career. He started the Carter

Center at Emory University 1982 where he and his supporters advocated for progressive issues like

human rights, free elections, clean air, and clean water. Over the last few decades, Carter has visited

Nicaragua to monitor their elections (1990) and was awarded the Nobel Peace Prize in 2002 for his

tireless humanitarian work. Four presidents have won the Nobel Peace Prize: Theodore Roosevelt,

Wilson, Carter, and Barack Obama. However, Carter won the prize after he was president.

Jimmy Carter 39th President of the United States (January 20, 1977,
to January 20, 1981) http://www.history.com/topics/us-presidents/Jimmy Carter/
pictures

The 40th President: Ronald Reagan

Ronald Reagan was the 40th president of the United States (January 20, 1981-January 20, 1989).

Born: February 6, 1911

Tampico, Illinois

Died: June 5, 2004 (aged 93)

Bel Air, Los Angeles, California

Education: Ronald Reagan graduated from Eureka College in 1932. Bachelor's degree

A former radio, television and movie actor and governor of California, Reagan came into office as the oldest American president (age 70), and promising a new era of optimism in America, after the darkness of the Carter years. However, just two months into his presidency, Reagan was shot by John Hinckley, on March 30, 1981. Hinckley had a crush on actress Jodie Foster, who refused to answer his letters, and he thought killing Reagan was a way to get the actress's attention. Hinckley was apprehended on the spot and spent many years in a mental institution. He was released just recently.

Reagan, whose wound was life-threatening, later joked with his wife, "Honey, I forgot to duck." He did, however, make a full recovery and served two terms as President.

Presidential Election of 1980

After the disappointment of the Iran Hostage Crisis and Carter's subsequent unpopularity, Ronald Reagan crushed President Jimmy Carter in the electoral count, 489 to 49. This was one of the largest presidential election wins for a presidential challenger against an incumbent in American history, and

Reagan warned that as soon as he was in office, he would end the hostage crisis, and Carter was worried that he might resort to using nuclear weapons. After the election, Carter's State Department worked hard with the Iranians who had taken the American hostages. At the very moment Reagan was taking the oath of office to become president, the hostages were released.

Presidential Election of 1984

During the 1984 presidential election, Reagan crushed his Democratic rival Walter Mondale even worse than he had President Carter in 1980. In the electoral votes Reagan won 525 to Mondale's 13, and took 18 million more votes than Mondale in the popular vote. Reagan's second presidential win was one of the largest both in electoral votes and popular votes.

Reagan's Domestic Policies

Reagan signs the Economic Tax Recovery Act of 1981 (August 13, 1981)

Reagan's first legislative push once he took office was for a tax cut to improve the lagging economy. He asked Congress to cut taxes by 30 percent; Congress agreed to cut taxes by 25 percent. Democratic critics were unsure what effect he would have on the U.S. economy. Between 1981 and 1982, the recession deepened, and Reagan's economic plan, Reaganomics, came to be called "Supply Side Economics." This economic theory looks at the economy as a whole (macroeconomics) and says that the best way to expand the economy is to lower marginal tax rates and reduce government regulations. The other four primary ideas of Reaganomics were: lower government spending, lower individual income taxes and capital gains taxes, decreasing government regulation, and restricting the money supply in the U.S.

to reduce inflation.

Other Effects on the Economy

On August 3, 1981, the Professional Air Traffic Controllers Union (PATCO) went on strike for better working conditions and a 32-hour work week. However, as federal employees, they were not allowed to strike by law. President Reagan told the air traffic controllers that their strike would cause a national emergency, and if they did not go back to work within two days, he would fire them. Out of 13,000 air traffic controllers, only 1,300 (10 percent) reported to work within the two-day deadline. Reagan fired 11,345 air traffic controllers on August 5, 1981 and banned them for life from federal employment. After the firing, strikes by federal employees fell dramatically.

Reagan and his wife First Lady Nancy Reagan came up with the anti-drug campaign, just 'say no' because both believed that drugs were a threat to American society, especially children and teenagers. In 1986, Reagan signed the Anti-Drug Abuse Act, which gave the war on drugs an additional $1.7-billion to fight drugs. He also made longer mandatory sentences for the possession of drugs. Reagan also appointed the first woman justice to the U.S. Supreme Court, Sandra Day O'Connor.

Reagan's Foreign Policy

Throughout his presidency, Reagan pursued the Reagan Doctrine, in which the U.S. supported the struggles of people across the globe against communist aggression. Reagan labeled the USSR an 'evil empire' on March 8, 1983 and pursued a policy of 'peace through strength', building up the American nuclear arsenal to the point where it was well beyond the Soviet capacity.

Tensions were high for years between the Soviet Union and the U.S. However, when Mikhail

Gorbachev became the general secretary of the U.S.S.R. in 1985 at age fifty-four, Gorbachev was one of the youngest Soviet leaders and was willing to work with Reagan. Between 1985 and 1988, Reagan and Gorbachev met at four international conferences. In 1987, these two world leaders signed the Intermediate-Range Nuclear Forces Treaty (INF), which resulted in over 2,000 missiles, both nuclear and conventional, being destroyed. Reagan also pushed in 1983 for the Strategic Defense Initiative, or Star Wars, where the U.S. could launch satellites in orbit around the world and shoot down Soviet nuclear missiles in case of World War III. Critics of this program included scientists who said the technology was not advanced enough to make it feasible to create a network of satellites in space.

However, the Soviet Union was already engaged in an arms race with the U.S. on nuclear weapons, as well as tanks and naval ships. The talk of 'Star Wars' added another financial burden to the Soviet Union that the Soviets could not really afford at this time and so they may have been more willing to negotiate with the U.S. on arms deals. President Reagan was also known for the dramatic moment when he stood in front of the Berlin Wall, which divided East and West Germany between 1961 and 1989. President Reagan addressed the Soviet leader Mikhail Gorbachev directly and called for him to, "Tear down this wall!" on June 12, 1987. The reaction from the German crowd was enthusiastic. When the Berlin Wall did come down on November 9, 1989, Reagan had already left office, but his enormous influence was a major factor in dismantling communism in countries around the world. Reagan also worked out an agreement with the Soviet Union in April 1988, that allowed Soviet troops to voluntarily withdraw from Afghanistan.

The biggest scandal of Reagan's administration was the Iran-Contra Affair, which involved the National Security Advisor (NSA) Robert McFarlane giving permission for the sale of anti-air missiles and anti-tank weapons to Hezbollah, a paramilitary terrorist group in Lebanon, in exchange for American hostages being held by Shia Muslims. The money generated from this sale, $48-million, went partly to help the Contras, who were engaged in a rebellion against the Sandinista government in Nicaragua. Such actions were illegal, but by using these funds through back channels, people in the Reagan administration could help the Contras. The sale happened in 1985, and the story came out in 1986. There were always allegations that both Reagan and Vice-President George Herbert Walker Bush knew about the affair, but this was never officially proven. The only people ever tried for this affair were Admiral Poindexter and Lieutenant Colonel Oliver North. North had immunity in exchange for his testimony and could not be convicted; Poindexter was pardoned by President Bush. No one went to jail for the Iran-Contra affair.

Ronald Reagan 40th President of the United States (January 20, 1981, to
    January 20, 1989) http://www.history.com/topics/us-presidents/Ronald Reagan/
    pictures

The 41st President: George Herbert Walker Bush

George Herbert Walker Bush was the 41st president of the United States (January 20, 1989-January 20, 1993).

Born: June 12, 1924 (aged 93)

Milton, Massachusetts

Education: Yale University: Bachelor's degree.

Political Party Affiliation: Republican

Bush's Domestic Policy

President Bush was elected to preside over the 'third term' of the very popular Ronald Reagan. With Congressional approval, he was signed the Americans with Disabilities Act of 1990, to grant the handicapped more rights when they either rented or owned a property that was their permanent residence. Now, if a handicapped person rented a property, the owner of the rental property was responsible for making sure that the property had wheelchair ramps installed so the renter could safely and easily get inside. The Cleaner Air Act of 1990 gave government agencies such as the EPA the right to pass laws or ordinances if they felt that a coal corporation was not doing enough to keep its plant clean and dumping chemicals into nearby rivers and streams.

Gregory D. Watson, a congressional aide, was the driving force to have the 27th constitutional amendment passed on May 22, 1992. This legislation was originally proposed back during the debate over the Bill of Rights in 1789! Watson discovered it while doing a school project and made it his quest for the next ten years, until by 1992 he had the necessary 38 U.S States to pass it. The amendment does not allow Congress to vote itself a pay raise while in session. When the amendment was finally passed,

it was 202 years old!

President Bush's biggest mistake was his pledge during the 1988 presidential campaign: "Read my lips: no new taxes". When he later went back on his pledge, this killed his credibility with the American public and was probably one of the reasons that he lost to Bill Clinton in the 1992 presidential election. The bill that raised taxes was the Omnibus Reconciliation Act of 1990, signed by President Bush on November 5, 1990. The bill raised taxes on the top income brackets from 28 percent to 31 percent; it also raised the marginal tax rate from 21 percent to 24 percent; it placed exorbitant taxes of 30% on luxury items such as $30,000.00 cars and $100,000.00 yachts. In theory, yacht owners would pay a total of 130,000.00 to buy a $100,000 yacht. This rolled back a lot of the gains from the Reagan years.

Bush's Foreign Policy

On November 9, 1989, the Berlin Wall came down. This was the wall that had separated West and East Germany since 1961 (during the Kennedy Administration); the dismantling of the wall led directly to the eventual dissolution of both East and West Germany by 1990 and paved the way to unite both halves of Germany for the first time since the end of World War II.

Chinese authorities cracked down on protesters at Tiananmen Square on June 4, 1989. All around the globe, the old order of communism began to collapse, country by country, week by week. A group of hard liners even kidnapped Gorbachev and placed him under house arrest from August 18, 1991 to August 21, 1991 in his Crimea home trying to get Gorbachev to resign; he refused to do so. Boris Yeltsin took to the streets of Moscow to protest and thousands of supporters joined Yeltsin. The attempted coup d'état collapsed of its own accord in three days.

On August 2, 1990, Saddam Hussein's Iraqi military forces invaded Kuwait. The Bush administration saw this as a direct threat to the oil supply of the U.S. President Bush went to the United Nations and asked for a charter supporting military action if diplomacy failed in dealing with Hussein and his takeover of Kuwait. President Bush built a coalition of Arab nations in the region; Saudi Arabia told Bush it was okay for the U.S. to send military forces there to protect it from possible invasion by Iraq, which the U.S. did. When diplomacy failed, the U.S. invaded Kuwait under the military operation Desert Storm on January 15, 1991.

The U.S. military aircraft bombed Iraq military forces for over a month. When the president finally authorized a ground offensive, the U.S. ground forces went on the offensive for only 100 hours before the president ordered a cease-fire; the objective had been achieved when Iraqi military forces had been driven out of Kuwait on February 28th, 1991. The commanding general was Norman Schwarzkopf, and the military forces used to launch this attack against Saddam Hussein numbered as many as 750,000 men and women. The Iraqi army may have had as many as 545,000 men in Kuwait when the battle began on January 15, 1991. This battle compared in size to the Battle of the Bulge between the Germans and the Allies in 1945, where there were over a million men involved.

George Herbert Walker Bush 41st President (January 20, 1989 to January 20, 1993)
http://cdn.loc.gov/service/pnp/cph/3b40000/3b46000/3b46100/3b46147v.jpg

The 42nd President: Bill Clinton

William Jefferson Clinton was the 42nd president of the United States (January 20, 1993-January 20, 2001).

Born: August 19, 1946 (aged 71)

Hope, Arkansas

Education: President Clinton graduated from Hot Springs, Arkansas High School in 1964. He graduated from Georgetown University Foreign Service School in 1968. President Clinton attended Oxford College in England as a Rhodes Scholar in 1969-1970, but never finished a degree program. He attended Yale Law School between 1970 and 1973 and graduated with a law degree in 1973. (Doctor of Jurisprudence). While at Yale he met his future wife, Hillary Rodham. They married on October 11, 1975.

The 1992 Presidential Election

President Clinton won only 43 percent of the popular vote, but he felt that this gave him a mandate to carry out his agenda for the American people. Ross Perot, an immensely popular third-party candidate, siphoned off many voters that would have normally have voted for Bush; this allowed Clinton to win.

Perot won more popular votes than any third-party candidate in the last eighty years, though he dropped out of the race, temporarily and inexplicably, about halfway through, and came back at the very end. Had he stayed in from beginning to end, he might well have won.

The 1996 Presidential Election

Incumbent Democratic president Bill Clinton won re-election with 379 electoral votes. His Republican challenger, Bob Dole, had 159 electoral votes. Ross Perot, who ran again as the Reform Party challenger, won less than half the popular votes he won in the 1992 presidential election. Clinton won this rather easily because the economy was doing well, and the world political situation was relatively stable.

Clinton's Domestic Policy

Clinton became president while America was in the middle of another recession, and his campaign internally stressed, "It's the economy, stupid". There was a budget debate in the U.S. Congress over how much money should be raised. President Clinton did support the largest tax bill in history, with approximately $500 billion to be spent to bring down the deficit and cutbacks in spending on the U.S. military too.

Clinton also promoted acceptance of gays in the U.S. military with his 'Don't ask, Don't tell' policy in 1994. Congress passed the Family Medical Leave Act on February 2, 1993, which gave employees up to twelve weeks of unpaid leave in a 12-month period—with their job security protected—for specific family and medical reasons. However, the American people did not approve of all the domestic actions that president Clinton took. In 1994, both Houses of Congress became Republican for the first time in 40 years. Now, President Clinton had to spend more time negotiating with the Republican Speaker of the House, Newt Gingrich and talking about the Contract with America that Gingrich insisted his Congress would pass.

Clinton did have a number of successes with the domestic economy: he reduced the deficit by half, according to many economists. He was able to generate as many as 22 million new jobs. Because of his increased hiring of police officers, the crime rate did fall in America during his Administration. More blacks and Latino and other minority workers were hired during his Administration. Clinton's economics were to establish fiscal discipline and eliminate the budget deficit; maintain low interest rates and encourage private-sector investments; eliminate protective tariffs; and invest in workers through education and research.

President Clinton's Foreign Policy

Failure to Win in Somalia

Clinton's predecessor, George Herbert Walker Bush, had ordered 28,000 U.S. military personnel to war-torn Somalia in eastern Africa on December 5, 1992, to aid the starving Somalians that military warlords refused to supply with food because they wanted the food to feed their own armies. The U.S. mission was "Operation Restore Hope", and the mission did save thousands of Somalian lives. However, when President Clinton took office on January 20, 1993, he expanded the mission to nation building. This did not turn out well; the U.S. was unable to restore order in this civil war. On October 3, 1993, forces in Somalia engaged U.S. military forces in their capital, Mogadishu, and in the ensuing 15-hour battle, two U.S. helicopters were downed. Although the U.S. was able to extract its forces, 18 U.S. soldiers were killed and another 73 wounded. Many American were shocked when the Somalis dragged dead U.S. soldiers though the streets of Mogadishu after the battle. After the battle, President Clinton decided to withdraw U.S. forces over several months. This encouraged terrorists such as Osama Bin Laden, who saw the withdrawal of American forces from Somalia as a sign of weakness.

President Clinton's Failure to Arrest Bin Laden

Whose fault is it that Bin Laden was not arrested in 1996? It depends whom you ask.

The Sudanese government wanted better foreign relations with the U.S., so they offered to hand over Osama Bin Laden (Bin Laden had been living in the capital of Sudan at Khartoum from 1991-1996). Clinton and his subordinates knew that Bin Laden was a terrorist mastermind, but they did not believe that they had enough evidence to hold him in April 1996. (The bombings of U.S. embassies in both in Kenya and Tanzania, credited to bin Laden, did not occur until August 7, 1998).

President Clinton and his staff wanted Saudi Arabia to take Osama back and put pressure on Saudi officials for several weeks to do so, but the Saudis refused. Eventually Osama was deported; he went to Afghanistan in 1996, and the Sudanese government seized many of his financial assets. The 9/11 Commission stated in its Report that they found no evidence of a deal for the Sudanese to give Osama to the U.S, though Lawrence Wright, author of THE LOOMING TOWER, claims there was a legitimate offer from the Sudanese to turn over bin Laden, and President Clinton refused.

President Clinton also invited Israeli Prime Minister Ehud Barak and Palestinian leader Yasser Arafat to Camp David on 7/11/2000, to try to resolve their differences, but nothing came of the meeting.

President Clinton's Successes in Foreign Policy

Peace in Northern Ireland & Peace between the Serbs, Croatians, and Muslims in the Balkans

President Clinton urged Catholics and Protestants to use diplomacy instead of violence to come to a peace agreement. Two years later, on April 10,1998, the Good Friday Peace Accords were signed in Northern Ireland between the Protestants and Catholic leaders, giving peace a real chance to happen. In Northern Ireland there had been violence between Catholics and the Protestants at least since 1969.

President Clinton was credited with getting the two parties together to work out this accord.

Starting on August 30, 1995, NATO, backed by American forces, hit Serbian forces for two weeks to get the Serbs to the negotiating table. The Dayton Peace Accords were signed on November 21, 1995, in which the countries of Bosnia and Herzegovina, Croatia, and Serbia agree to end hostilities. Over 250,000 have died in the fighting in four years. More than two million refugees fled from the fighting. This is an important first step in the road to peace.

President Clinton's Legacy

The biggest mistake that President Bill Clinton committed while in public office—and which forever defined his presidency--was his affair with a White House intern, 22-year-old Monica Lewinsky, from 1995 to early 1997.

This affair led to his indictment by special prosecutor Ken Starr, who turned over the evidence he collected to a Congressional committee. Then the U.S. House of Representatives began the impeachment process by gathering evidence against the president, eventually charging him with perjury and obstruction of justice. The U.S. Senate tried the president (the first impeachment trial in the Senate since Andrew Johnson was tried in the 1860's) and acquitted him of perjury on February 12,

1999: 55-45. The vote on obstruction was 50-50. For the president to be removed from public office the vote would have to have been 67 votes or 2/3 in favor.

However, Clinton's affair with Monica Lewinsky, along with the other revelations of his tawdry extramarital sex life, remained the largest part of his presidential legacy.

There were numerous scandals during the Clinton Administration, including the suspicious 'suicide' of presidential counselor Vince Foster, a Clinton friend since age six, in the summer of 1993. There was the attack on the compound at Waco, Texas when a group of cultists were driven out, with many,

including children, killed in the attack. There was the Whitewater scandal, with the Clintons at the center of a failed land scheme in which they made money, but hundreds of others lost a fortune.

Bill Clinton 42nd President of the United States
(January 20, 1993 to January 20, 2001)
http://cdn.loc.gov/service/pnp/cph/3c00000/3c07000/3c07700/3c07700v.jpg

The 43rd President: George Bush

George Walker (W.) Bush was the 43rd president of the United States (January 20, 2001-January 20, 2009).

Born: July 6, 1941 (aged 71)

New Haven, Connecticut

Political Party Affiliation: Republican

Family Background:

Parental History: His father is George Herbert Walker Bush (June 12, 1924-present) and his mother is Barbara Bush (June 8, 1925-present).

George Walker (W.) Bush is married to Laura Bush, a librarian (1977). They have twin daughters, Barbara and Jenna.

George Bush is only the second president (like John Quincy Adams) who was also the son of a former president.

Education: George Bush went to the elite prep school Andover, then to Yale university where he earned an undergraduate degree in History (1968). He went on to Harvard Business School where he earned a Master of Business Administration (MBA) in 1975.

Presidential Election of 2000

This was possibly the closest-ever presidential election in which George W. Bush, the son of former president George H. W. Bush and governor of Texas, ran against Al Gore, Jr. (son of a Tennessee senator, a Democratic Senator himself, and then vice-president to Bill Clinton). Bush won 271 electoral votes and 50,456,062 popular votes. Gore won 266 electoral votes and half a million more popular votes. After calling the state of Florida for Bush early on Election Night, the media reversed itself and said it was too close to call, and the entire state had to be recounted to determine who won its 25 electoral votes.

After weeks of recounting, the case went to the U.S. Supreme Court, which found in Bush's favor. (Bush v. Gore, 2000) on December 12, 2000. Many people felt Bush had 'stolen' the election from Al Gore and regarded Bush as an illegitimate president throughout his two terms in office.

Presidential Election of 2004

The incumbent George W. Bush won the presidential election of 2004 with 286 electoral votes; his Democratic challenger, Senator John F. Kerry, had 251 electoral votes. There was some speculation that there was voter irregularity in Ohio, and if Kerry had won Ohio, he would have won the election, but Kerry decided not to make an issue of it. Bush was declared the winner of the 2004 presidential election.

Bush's Domestic Policy

Bush enacted the Medicare description drug benefit, which made drugs cheaper to senior citizens by promoting competition. President Bush also help enact "No Child Left Behind", which was created to help minority students perform better on tests. As governor of Texas, Bush had created a successful version of this program; implementing it nationwide was one of his most important reasons for running for president. Unfortunately, it was not nearly as successful at the federal level.

9/11

Bush had barely begun his presidency when on Tuesday, September 11, 2001, four commercial airplanes were hijacked in the early morning at airports in New York and Boston. These planes, taken over by nineteen Middle-Eastern young men, radicalized and trained as members of Al-Qaeda, a radical terrorist organization, and armed only with box cutters, were re-routed in the air. Two of the planes, one from American Airlines, one from United Airlines, slammed into the Twin Towers of New York City's World Trade Center. One smashed into the side of the Pentagon.

The fourth, United 93, headed back to Washington, D.C. from Pennsylvania. The passengers, realizing a major terrorist attack was taking place, voted to retake the plane and actually attacked the hijackers. They had control of the plane when it smashed into the ground at Shanksville, Pennsylvania. Everyone on board was killed.

The Twin Towers, built to withstand even the crash of a 747 into the building, could not withstand the intense heat of the jet-fuel fires burning within them. Within a single hour, both towers, with hundreds of people inside, fell to the ground, straight into their own footprints. Later that day, Building 7 in the World Trade Center complex also fell. Of the hundreds trapped inside, only twenty were rescued from the ruins of the building; the rest died.

The attack against America on 9/11 was the single worst attack on American soil since Pearl Harbor, with almost 3000 people dying in one morning. It was a day that profoundly changed how Americans thought about their country. After this day, Americans were furious and grief-stricken. They were ready to go to war. And Osama bin Laden, who was blamed for inspiring the attacks, became America's #1 enemy. The hunt for him became immediate, intense and overwhelming. It would continue for years.

Bush's Foreign Policy

Bush (43) had information from the CIA that the leader of Iraq, Saddam Hussein, who had once taken over Kuwait and forced the Gulf War, now had weapons of mass destruction and was working on nuclear weapons. President Bush used this as an official reason for invading Iraq.

He went to the U.N. to get justification for this invasion, and the U.S. Congress also authorized the president to use force. On March 21, 2003, Bush launched Operation Iraqi Freedom; U.S forces invaded Iraq to overthrow Saddam and his regime. Regrettably, though U.S. forces easily conquered Saddam (he was later executed by Iraqis), the military found itself in a quagmire that the U.S. never seems to be able to leave completely, because our actions have de-stabilized the region.

Bush upset his critics by withdrawing from the Kyoto accords, which were signed in Japan in 1997. This treaty was designed by supporters of global warming with rigid requirements on U.S. industry to lower emission standards. China and India were excluded from this agreement.

Another decision with domestic repercussions was enhanced interrogation methods, including waterboarding, where water is poured on the person to simulate drowning. Supporters say such methods were necessary to gather vital intelligence and information and save lives, which could otherwise be lost to terrorism. Critics say that it made the U.S. no better than the terrorists that the U.S. was fighting.

Others called Bush a staunch supporter of Israel. Bush also provided $15 billion in aid to the poor in Africa, one of the regions hit hardest by the AIDS epidemic.

Bush made a quick response to the 9/11 attacks by Al-Qaida by putting U.S. forces on offensive in Afghanistan by October 7, 2001. At the end of his presidency he also preserved marine life with

195,280 square miles set aside for three national monuments.

Bush also made an unpopular decision when he decided to send an additional 30,000 troops to Iraq, lessening the violence in Iraq at least for a time, while American troops were there. Bush also removed the Taliban, a brutal repressive regime, in Afghanistan. Unfortunately, there does not seem to be any long-term exit strategy to get Americans out of either Iraq or Afghanistan. The mere fact that the United States and its military are still in Afghanistan (since 2001) and in Iraq (since 2003) have led some critics to claim that the United States has not only invaded two sovereign countries but has also engaged (unsuccessfully) in nation building, too.

George Walker Bush 43rd President of the United States
(January 20, 2001 to January 20, 2009)
http://cdn.loc.gov/service/pnp/ppbd/00300/00371v.jpg

The 44th President of the United States: Barack Obama

Barack Hussein Obama was the 44th president of the United States (January 20, 2009-January 20, 2017).

Born: August 4, 1961 (aged 56)

Honolulu, Hawaii

Political Party Affiliation: Democrat

Though he had a white mother and a black father and is therefore only half-black, Barack Obama is considered our first black president, a milestone in the history of the presidency.

Family Background:

Parental History: His parents are Barack Hussein Obama Sr. (1936-1982) and Ann Durham (1942-1995). Barack's father was born in Nynaza Province, Kenya. His mother was originally from Wichita, Kansas. His parents moved to Honolulu, Hawaii, where Barack Jr. was born on August 4, 1961. Later his parents split up, with his father moving back to Kenya. Barack's mom later married an Indonesian man, Lolo Soetero, who lived and worked in Indonesia, as did Barack and his mother, for some years. Barack was eventually sent to live with his maternal grandparents in Hawaii.

Barack Obama's Marriage: Barack married Michelle Robinson on October 3, 1992. They have two daughters, Malia (19) and Sasha (17).

Education: Punahou college prep school in Honolulu, Hi. Graduated with honors in 1979.

After high school, he studied at Occidental College for two years and transferred to Columbia University in 1983 after acquiring a degree in Political Science and English literature. Graduated from Harvard Law School in 1991.

President Barack Obama published a book, *Dreams from My Father: A Story of Race and Inheritance,* in 1995, which dealt with his father's advice on life and how both he and his father dealt with racism. Obama also wrote *The Audacity of Hope: Thoughts on Reclaiming the American Dream,* which was published in 2006. This work presented his political views on American society and how he can shape the future of American politics.

Political Activism

Early in his career, Barack Obama worked on the south side of Chicago as a community organizer, trying to make a better life for the poor residents of Chicago. After graduating from Columbia, Obama worked in the Development of the Communities Project from 1985 - 1988, where he created job-training programs, a college tutoring program, and a tenants' rights organization. After Obama graduated from Harvard law school in 1991, he became a civil rights attorney and professor where he not only worked for the poor, but he was also a professor and taught civil-rights law at the University of Chicago Law School, from 1992-2004.

Legislative Career

In 1996, Obama was elected a state senator of Illinois, serving three terms, from 1997 to 2004. He won the U.S. Senate race in 2005 and began to plan a run for the presidency. Obama won the Democratic nomination for U.S. President in 2008 and defeated the Republican nominee, John McCain, that November.

Obama's Legislative and Domestic Policy

During his first term (2009-2013), Congress passed The Patient Protection and Affordable Care Act, also known as Obamacare. They also passed the Dodd-Frank Wall Street and Consumer Protection Act, the Don't Ask, Don't Tell Repeal Act of 2010, the American Recovery and Reinvestment Act of 2009, the Tax Relief and Unemployment Reauthorization Act, and the Job Creation Act of 2010.

Obama's Legislative and Domestic Policy

In his second term, Obama pushed for more rights for homosexuals and lesbians, working through the Lesbian, Gay, Bisexual and Transgendered (LGBT) group. He pushed for the U.S. Supreme Court to make gay marriage legal. But there were moments of great violence as well.

On December 14, 2012, a shooting occurred at the Sandy Hook Elementary School in Newton, Connecticut, in which 20 children were shot and killed. Six staff members were shot as well by Adam Lanza, a 20-year-old man who took his own life when police arrived on the scene.

In reaction to the Sandy Hook shooting, President Obama signed 23 executive orders on January 13, 2013, some of which limited the amount of ammunition magazines could carry to ten rounds per magazine. Some orders reinstated the expired ban on assault weapons, and he also banned the possession and sale of armor-piercing rounds.

Obama's Foreign Policy

During his first term (2009-2013), President Obama ordered the withdrawal of U.S. troops from Iraq, though he had to send back troops to Iraq in 2011 when a new terrorist organization, ISIS, started making political and material gains in Iraq. He ordered an increase in troops in Afghanistan and also ordered U.S. military involvement in Libya against Muammar Qaddafi, which unseated the dictator and destabilized the entire Middle East as a result. He also negotiated nuclear reductions with the Russians through the Start Treaty. He also had Osama Bin Laden killed by a U.S. Navy seal team on May 2, 2011. And just weeks before the 2012 election, the Ambassador to Libya, Christopher Stevens, was killed in Benghazi by a terrorist attack on the compound, along with three others, including two CIA contractors who came to help in 1 13-hour firefight when no one else would.

Barack Obama (January 20, 2009 to January 20, 2017)
http://cdn.loc.gov/service/pnp/ppbd/00600/00603v.jpg

The 45th President of the United States: Donald J. Trump

Donald John Trump is the 45th president of the United States, inaugurated on January 20, 2017.

Born: June 14, 1946 (aged 71)

Queens, New York

Education: When Donald Trump was thirteen, he was sent to military school, from which he graduated in 1964. He went on to Fordham University, and two years later transferred to the prestigious Wharton School of Business at the University of Pennsylvania, from which he graduated in 1968 with a degree in economics.

Political Party Affiliation: Republican

Family Background: His parents are Fred and Mary Anne MacLeod Trump. He is the fourth of five children. His father made a fortune building middle-priced apartment housing in the real-estate boom in the 1950s. His father passed away in 1999; his mother passed away in 2000.

Trump came into office as the oldest American president, being a few months older than Ronald Reagan was when he assumed the Presidency.

Trump has been married three times: to Ivana Zelnickova (1977-1992), with whom he had three children: Donald Junior, born in 1977, Ivanka, born in 1981, and Eric, born in 1984; to Marla Maples (1993-1997), with whom he had a daughter Tiffany, named after the world-famous jewelry company; and to model Melania Knauss, whom he married in January 2005; their son Barron was born in March 2006.

Business & Celebrity Fame:

Trump over many years in business has earned a net worth valued at $3.1-billion (in 2017). This fortune was in New York real estate, golf clubs, casinos and other businesses; he became famous as a builder of Manhattan buildings; Trump Tower on Fifth Avenue is the best-known.

Trump is the wealthiest man ever to become president of the United States. He is blunt and outspoken, not afraid to express his views in public, and especially on his own television reality shows: *The Apprentice*, which began in 2004, and *Celebrity Apprentice*, both wildly popular with television audiences. (Trump earned a star on Hollywood Boulevard for his efforts and was nominated for an Emmy Award.) Show contestants competed with their business skills to win jobs in the Trump Organization. On *Celebrity Apprentice*, celebrity contestants competed for prize money donated to their favorite charities.

Presidential Election

Donald Trump had talked for years about running for president and almost ran in 2012 but decided not to run at that time. After Mitt Romney, the Republican nominee in 2012, lost to Barack Obama, Trump quietly trademarked the phrase "Make America Great Again", and began to prepare for a run in 2016.

2016 was one of the most contentious and divisive campaigns ever staged, with Trump running first against 16 other Republican candidates, whom he beat easily in the Republican primaries. His theme of "Make America Great Again" resonated with voters, who turned out by the thousands to hear him at massive rallies all over the country. After he won the nomination (the first non-military, non-politician ever to do so), Trump faced off against Hillary Clinton, former First Lady to ex-President Bill Clinton, former Senator from New York, former Secretary of State (under Barack Obama), and expected to easily win and become the nation's first woman president.

But Trump's message of "Make America Great Again" and oft-repeated promise to build a wall on the southern border of the U.S. to prevent illegal immigrants from getting into the country resonated with voters all over the country, who were sick of the corruption in Washington and the contempt the governing class had for them. After a vicious and bitter fall campaign, on November 8, 2016, Trump won the election with 306 electoral votes to Clinton's 232. This win was possibly the most surprising in American political history, which immediately led to protests and riots all over the country, as angry Clinton voters refused to accept Trump's victory and vowed to resist his presidency for every day it lasted. At the same time, right after Trump won the election, the stock market hit 20,000 for the first time in history, followed by new highs every month. In early January 2018, it broke a new record, getting to 26,000 for the first time.

In Trump's first year in office, he focused on trying to repeal Obamacare (which didn't happen though he did get rid of parts of it), take better care of military veterans through our military hospitals (which he did), defeat ISIS overseas (which was largely decimated by the end of the year), prevent immigration from countries which sponsored terrorism in the Middle East (which the Supreme Court finally allowed him to do), grow the economy through rolling back unnecessary regulations (which he did), bring back jobs from American companies who built factories in other countries (he did) and appoint a new Supreme Court justice to fill the seat vacated by Justice Anthony Scalia, who died in 2016. He appointed Justice Neil Gorsuch at the very beginning of his term.

In December 2017, at his urging, Congress passed one of the most comprehensive tax-reform bills in American history. He also set the record for number of federal appeals courts judges confirmed by the Senate in his first year (12). But Trump's presidency has been marred by accusations that he

colluded with Russian agents to rig and then steal the 2016 election from Hillary Clinton. In June 2017,

Robert Mueller, former head of the FBI, was appointed as special counsel to investigate these claims.

As of this writing, there is no evidence at all that Trump tried to collude with the Russians to steal the

election, and Mueller has announced that there is no evidence that any American knowingly tried to rig

the election. However, there is mounting evidence now that Hillary Clinton paid for a salacious dossier

to be created about Trump, which could be used as opposition research and was later used to obtain a

warrant to spy on him before, during, and after the election.

Donald Trump President of the United States
(January 20, 2017 to the Present time).
http://cdn.loc.gov/service/pnp/ppbd/00600/00608v.jpg

Conclusion

The Physical Expansion of the United States & Assassinated U.S. Presidents

In 1776, the total square footage of the thirteen colonies was 430,000 square miles. Today, the square footage of the fifty states United States is 3.797 million square miles. Part of this growth was caused by the nineteenth-century belief in Manifest Destiny—Americans' right to expand their territory from East Coast to West Coast. The American population has grown from four million Americans in the first census in 1790 to 324,000,000 in 2017. Again, there have been forty-four men who have been president (Grover Cleveland is the only president who served two non-consecutive terms, March 4, 1885 to March 4, 1889 and March 4, 1893 to March 4, 1897). However, there have been forty-five terms that men have served as President of the United States since the founding of the American Republic.

Four Presidential Assassinations

Four presidents died by assassination while in office: Lincoln in 1865 (John Wilkes Booth); James Garfield in 1881 (Charles Guiteau); William McKinley in 1901; (Leon Czolgosz); John Fitzgerald Kennedy in 1963 (Lee Harvey Oswald, accused but never tried or convicted).

Three Attempted Assassinations on U.S. Presidents

Three presidents have had attempted assassinations while in office: The first attempt was by Richard

Lawrence attempted to execute Andrew Jackson in 1835 but both of his pistols misfired; The second attempt was on Gerald Ford and on two separate occasions two different women tried to assassinate President Gerald Ford while the president was in California; The first attempt was on September 5, 1975, Lynnete 'Squeakie" Fromme tried to kill the president while he was in Sacramento, California but the Secret Service quickly disarmed her. The second time was on September 22, 1975, while in San Francisco a woman named Sara Jane Moore shot at the president twice, but a bystander Oliver Sipple blocked her second shot and the Secret Service quickly got the president pushed into a limousine and out of the area. The woman Mrs. Moore was quickly arrested. The third assassination attempt was committed by John Hinckley on Ronald Reagan in 1981 but failed, and Reagan had two full terms in office.

Theodore Roosevelt was not President when He was shot by John Schrank

On October 14, 1912, while campaigning for president, T.R. was shot by a madman named John Schrank. Schrank aimed for T.R.'s heart but T.R. survived because he had a fifty page speech report crammed in his shirt pocket, which incidentally stopped the bullet from penetrating his heart! Not only did T.R. survive the assassination attempt but he gave his scheduled speech before going to the hospital!

Finally, America has grown enormously, from thirteen original colonies in 1776 on the East Coast to an American colossus, with fifty states, millions of miles of land, and prodigious military and spending power. America still has many problems, including failing cities and towns, illegal aliens, deficit spending, and crumbling infrastructure. However, if President Trump controls immigration by building a wall on the Southern border, reduces spending in the U.S. Congress, and creates more jobs for the American people, then Americans will feel better about themselves and America, and he will leave office having truly kept his promise to 'Make America Great Again'.

Appendix I

The Declaration of Independence

When in the course of human events it becomes necessary for one people to dissolve the political bonds which have connected them with another and to assume the powers of the earth, the separate and equal stations, to which the Laws of Nature and Nature's God entitle them, a decent respect to the opinion of mankind requires that they should declare the causes which impel them to separation. We hold these truths to be self-evident, that all men are created equal, they are endowed by their Creator with certain unalienable Rights, among these are Life, Liberty, and the pursuit of Happiness.-That to secure these Rights, governments are instituted among Men deriving their just powers from the consent of the governed,- That whenever any Form of Government becomes destructive of these ends, it is the Right of the People to alter or abolish it, and to institute a new Government, laying its foundation on such principles and organizing its power in such form, as to that them shall seem to effect their Safety and Happiness. Prudence, indeed, will dictate that governments long established should not be changed for light and transient causes; and accordingly all experience have shewn that mankind are more disposed to suffer while evils are sufferable than to right themselves by abolishing the forms of to which they are accustomed. But when a long train of abuses and usurpations, pursuing invariably the same Object evinces a design to reduce them under absolute Despotism, it is their right, it is their duty, to throw off such Government, and to provide new Guards for their future security.-Such has been the patience sufferance of these Colonies; and such now is the necessity which constrains them to alter their former Systems of Government. The history of the present King of Great Britain is a history of repeated injuries and usurpations, all having in direct object the establishment of a direct Tyranny over these States. To prove this, let the Facts, be submitted to a candid world.

He has refused his Assent to the Laws, the most wholesome and necessary for the public good.

He has forbidden his Governors to pass Laws of immediate and pressing importance, unless suspended in their operation until his Assent should be obtained; and when so suspended he has utterly neglected to attend them

He has refused to pass laws for the accommodation of large districts of people, unless those people would relinquish the right of Representation in the Legislature, a right inestimable to them and formidable to tyrants only.

He has called legislative bodies in unusual places, uncomfortable, and distant form the depository of their Public Records, for the sole purpose of fatiguing into compliance with his measures.

He has dissolved many House of Representatives, for opposing with manly firmness his invasions on the rights of the people.

He has refused for a long time, after such dissolution, to cause others to be annihilated, whereby the Legislative Powers, incapable of annihilation, have returned to the People at large for their exercise; the State remaining in the mean time exposed to all the dangers of invasion from without, convulsions within.

He has endeavored to prevent population of these states; for the purpose of obstructing the Laws for Naturalization of Foreigners; refusing to pass others to encourage migration hither, and raising the new conditions of Appropriations of Lands.

He has obstructed the Administration of Justice by refusing his Assent to Laws for establishing new laws. He has made Judges dependent on his Will alone for the tenure of their offices, and the amount of payment of their salaries.

He has kept among us, in times of peace, Standing armies without the consent of our Legislatures.

He has affected to render the Military independent and superior to the Civil power.

He has combined with others to subject us with a jurisdiction that is foreign to our constitution, and unacknowledged by our laws; giving his Assent to their pretended Acts of Legislation:

For quartering large bodies of armed troops among us:

For protecting them, by a mock Trial for punishment for any Murders which they shall commit on the Inhabitants of these States:

For cutting off our Trade with all parts of the world:

For imposing Taxes without our Consent:

For depriving us in many cases, of the benefit by Trial of Jury:

For transporting us beyond the Seas, to be tried for pretended offenses:

For abolishing the free System of English Laws in a neighbouring Province establishing therein an Arbitrary government, and enlarging its boundaries so as to render it at once an example of and fit instrument for introducing the same absolute rule into these colonies.

For taking away our charters, abolishing our most valuable Laws, and altering fundamentally our Forms of Governments:

For suspending our own Legislatures, and declaring themselves invested with the power to legislate for us in all cases whatsoever.

He has abdicated Government here, by declaring us out of his Protection and waging War against us.

He has plundered our seas, ravaged our coasts, burnt our towns, and destroyed the lives of our people.

He is at this time transporting large Armies of foreign Mercenaries, to compleat the works of death, desolation, and tyranny, already begun with circumstances of Cruelty& Perfidy scarcely paralleled in the most barbarous ages, and totally unworthy of the Head of a civilized nation.

Constrained our fellow Citizens, taken captive on the high seas to bear arms against their Country, to become the executioner of their friends and Brethren, or to fall themselves by their hands.

He has excited domestic insurrections amongst us, and has endeavoured to bring on the inhabitants of our frontiers, the merciless Indian Savages whose known rule of warfare, is an undistinguished destruction of all ages, sexes, and conditions.

In every stage of these Oppressions We have Petitioned for Redress in the most humble terms: Our repeated Petitions have been answered only by repeated injuries. A Prince, whose character is thus marked by every act which may define a Tyrant, is unfit to be the ruler of a free people.

http://www.ushistory.org/declaration/document/

Nor have we been wanting in attention to our British Brethren. We have warned them from time to time of attempts by their legislature to extend an unwarrantable jurisdiction over us. We have reminded them of the circumstances of our emigration and settlement here. We have appealed to their native justice and magnanimity, and we have have conjured them by ties of our common kindred to disavow these usurpations, which, would, inevitably interrupt our connections and correspondence. We must, therefore, acquiesce in the necessity, which denounces our separation, and hold them, as we hold the rest of mankind, enemies in war, in peace friends.

We, therefore, the representatives of the United States of America, in General Congress, assembled, appealing to the Supreme Judge of the world for the rectitude of our intentions, do, in the name, and by the authority of the good people of the colonies, solemnly publish and declare, that these united colonies are, and of right ought to be free and independent states; that they are absolved from all allegiance to the British Crown, and that all political connection between them and the state of Great Britain, is and ought to be totally dissolved; and that as free and independent states, they have full power to levy war, conclude peace, contract alliances, establish commerce, and do all other acts and things which independent states may of right do. And for the support of this declaration, with a firm reliance on the protection of Divine Providence, we mutually pledge to each other our lives, our fortunes, and our sacred honor. http:/www.let.rug.nl/usa/documents/1776-1785/the-final-text-of-the-declaration-of-independence-july-4-1776.php

Appendix II

Transcript of Constitution of the United States (1787)

We the People of the United states, in Order to form a more perfect Union, establish Justice, insure domestic Tranquility, provide for the common defence, promote the general Welfare, and secure the Blessings of Liberty to ourselves and our Posterity, do ordain and establish this Constitution for the United States of America.

Article, I.

Section. 1.

All legislative powers herein granted shall be vested in a Congress of the United States, which shall consist of a Senate and House of Representatives.

Section. 2.

The House of Representatives shall be composed of Members chosen every second Year by the People of the several States, and the Electors in each State shall have the Qualifications requisite for Electors of the most numerous Branch of the State Legislature.

No Person shall be a Representative who shall not have attained to the Age of twenty five Years, and been seven Years a Citizen of the United States, and who shall not, when elected, be an Inhabitant of that State in which he shall be chosen.

Representatives and direct Taxes shall be apportioned among the several States which may be included within this Union, according to their respective Numbers, which shall be determined by adding to the whole Number of free Persons, including those bound to Service for a Term of Years, and excluding Indians not taxed, three fifths of all other Persons. The actual Enumeration shall be made within three Years after the first Meeting of the Congress of the United States, and within every subsequent Term of ten Years, in such Manner as they shall by Law direct. The Number of Representatives shall not exceed one for every thirty Thousand, but each State shall have at Least one Representative; and until such enumeration shall be made the State of New Hampshire shall be entitled to chuse three, Massachusetts eight, Rhode-Isalnd and Providence Plantations one, Connecticut five, New-York six, New Jersey four, Pennsylvania eight, Delaware one, Maryland six, Virginia ten, North Carolina five, South Carolina five, and Georgia three.

When vacancies happen in the Representation form any State, the Executive Authority thereof shall issue Writs of Election to fill such Vacancies.

The House of Representatives shall chuse their Speaker and other Officers; and shall have the sole Power of Impeachment.

Section. 3.

The Senate of the United States shall be composed of two Senators form each State, chosen by the

Legislature thereof, for six Years; and each Senator shall have one Vote.

Immediately after they shall be assembled in Consequence of the first Election, they shall be divided as equally as my be into three Classes. The Seats of the Senators of the first Class shall be vacated at the Expiration of the second Year, of the second Class at the Expiration of the fourth Year, and of the third Class at the Expiration of the sixth Year, so that one third may be chosen every second Year; and if Vacancies happen by Resignation, or otherwise, during the Recess of the Legislature of any State, the Executive thereof may make temporary Appointments unitl the next Meeting of the Legislature, which shall fill such Vacancies.

No Person shall be a Senator who shall not have attained to the Age of thirty Years, and been nine Years a Citizen of the United States, and who shall not, when elected, be an Inhabitant of that State for which he shall be chosen.

The Vice President of the United States shall be President of the Senate, but shall have no Vote, unless they be equally divided.

The Senate shall chuse their other Officers, and also a President pro tempore, in the Absence of the Vice President, or when he shall exercise the Office of President of the United States.

 The Senate shall have the sole Power to try all Impeachments. When sititng for that Purpose, they shall be on Oath or Affirmation. When the President of the United States is tried, the Chief Justice shall preside: And no Person shall be convicted without the Concurrence of two thirds of the Members present.

Judgment in Cases of Impeachment shall not extend further than to removal from Office, and disqualification to hold and enjoy any Office of honor, Trust or Profit under the United States: but the Party convicted shall nevertheless be liable and subject to Indictment, Trial, Judgment and Punishment, according to Law.

Section.4.

The Times, Places and Manner of holding Elections for Senators and Representatives, shall be prescribed in each state by the Legislature thereof; but the Congress may at any time by Law make or alter such Regulations, except as to the Places of chusing Senators.

The Congress shall assemble at least once in every Year, and such Meeting shall be on the first Monday in December, unless they by Law appoint a different Day.

Section. 5.

Each House shall be the Judge of the Elections, Returns and Qualifications of its own Members, and a Majority of each shall constitute a Quorum to do Business; but a smaller Number may adjourn from day to day, and may be authorized to compel the Attendance of absent Members, in such Manner, and under such Penalties as each House may provide.

Each House may determine the Rules of its Proceedings, punish its Members for disorderly Behaviour, and, with the Concurrence of tow thirds, expel a Member.

Each House shall keep a Journal of its Proceedings, and from time to time publish the same, excepting such Parts as may in their judgment require Secrecy; and the Yeas and Nays of the Members of either House on any question shall, at the Desire of one fifth of those Present, be entered on the Journal.

Neither House, during the Session of Congress, shall, without the Consent of the other, adjourn for more than three days, nor to any other Place than that in which the two Houses shall be sitting.

Section. 6.

The Senators and Representatives shall receive a Compensation for their Services, to be ascertained by Law, and paid out of the Treasury of the United States. They shall in all Cases, except Treason, Felony and Breach of the Peace, be privileged from Arrest during their Attendance at the Session of their respective Houses, and in going to and returning from the same; and for any Speech or Debate in either House, they shall not be questioned in any other Place.

No Senator or Representative shall, during the Time for which he was elected, be appointed to any civil Office under the Authority of the United States, which shall have been created, or the Emoluments whereof shall have been encreased during such time; and no Person holding any Office under the United States shall be a Member of either House during his Continuance in Office.

Section 7.

All Bills for raising Revenue shall originate in the House of Representatives; but the Senate may propose or concur with Amendments as on other Bills. Every Bill which shall have passed the House of Representatives and the Senate, shall, before it become a Law, be presented to the President of the United States If he approve; he shall sign it, but if not he shall return it, with his Objections to that House in which it shall have originated, who shall enter the Objections at large on their Journal, and proceed to reconsider it. If after such Reconsideration two thirds of that House shall agree to pass the Bill, it shall be sent, with the Objections, to the other House, by which it shall be likewise reconsidered, and if approved by two thirds of that House, it shall become a Law. But in all such Cases the Votes of both Houses shall be determined by yeas and Nays, and the Names of the Persons voting for and against the Bill shall be entered on the Journal of each House respectively. If any Bill shall not be returned by the President within ten Days (Sundays excepted) after it shall have been presented to him, the Same shall be a Law, in like Manner as if had signed it, unless the Congress by their Adjournment prevent its Return, in which Case it shall not be a Law.

Every Order, Resolution, or Vote to which the Concurrence of the Senate and House of Representatives may be necessary (except on a question of Adjournment) shall be presented to the President of the United States; and before the Same shall take Effect, shall be approved by him, or being disapproved by him, shall be repassed by two thirds of the Senate and House of Representatives, according to the Rules and Limitations prescribed in the Case of a Bill.

Section. 8.

The Congress shall have Power To lay and collect Taxes, Duties, Imposts and Excises, to pay the Debts and provide for the common Defence and general Welfare of the United States; but all Duties, Imposts and Excises shall be uniform throughout the United States;

To borrow Money on the credit of the United States;

To regulate Commerce with foreign Nations, and among the several States, and with the Indian Tribes;

To establish an uniform Rule of Naturalization, and uniform Laws on the subject of Bankruptcies throughout the United States;

To coin Money, regulate the Value thereof, and of foreign Coin, and fix the Standard of Weights and Measures;

To provide for the Punishment of counterfeiting the Securities and current Coin of the United States;

To establish Post Offices and post Roads;

To promote the Progress of Science and useful Arts, by securing for limited Times to Authors and Inventors the exclusive Right to their respective Writings and Discoveries;

To constitute Tribunals inferior to the supreme Court;

To define and punish Piracies and Felonies committed on the high Seas, and Offences against the Law of Nations;

To declare War, grant Letters of Marque and Reprisal, and make Rules concerning Captures on Land and Water;

To raise and support Armies, but no Appropriation of Money to that Use shall be for a longer Term than two Years;

To provide and maintain a Navy;

To make Rules for the Government and Regulation of the land and naval Forces;

To provide for calling forth the Militia to execute the Laws of the Union, suppress Insurrections and repel Invasions;

To provide for organizing, arming, and disciplining, the Militia, and for governing such Part of them as may be employed in the Service of the United States, reserving to the States respectively, the Appointment of the Officers, and the Authority of training the Militia according to the discipline prescribed by Congress;

To exercise exclusive Legislation in all Cases whatsoever, over such District (not exceeding ten Miles square) as may, by Cession of particular States, and the Acceptance of Congress, become the Seat of the Government of the United States, and to exercise like Authority over all Places purchased by the Consent of the Legislature of the State in which the Same shall be, for the Erection of Forts, Magazines, Arsenals, dockyards, and other needful Buildings;—And

To make all Laws which shall be necessary and proper for carrying into Execution the foregoing Powers, and all other Powers vested by this Constitution in the Government of the United States, or in any Department or Officer thereof.

Section. 9.

The Migration or Importation of such Persons as any of the States now existing shall think proper to admit, shall not be prohibited by the Congress prior to the Year one thousand eight hundred and eight, but a Tax or duty may be imposed on such Importation, not exceeding ten dollars for each Person.

The Privilege of the Writ of Habeas Corpus shall not be suspended, unless when in Cases of Rebellion or Invasion the public Safety may require it.

No Bill of Attainder or ex post facto Law shall be passed.

No Capitation, or other direct, Tax shall be laid, unless in Proportion to the Census or enumeration herein before directed to be taken.

No Tax or Duty shall be laid on Articles exported from any State.

No Preference shall be given by any Regulation of Commerce or Revenue to the Ports of one State over those of another: nor shall Vessels bound to, or from, one State, be obliged to enter, clear, or pay Duties in another.

No Money shall be drawn from the Treasury, but in Consequence of Appropriations made by Law; and a regular Statement and Account of the Receipts and Expenditures of all public Money shall be published from time to time.

No Title of Nobility shall be granted by the United States: And no Person holding any Office of Profit or Trust under them, shall, without the Consent of the Congress, accept of any present, Emolument, Office, or Title, of any kind whatever, from any King, Prince, or foreign State.

Section. 10.

No State shall enter into any Treaty, Alliance, or Confederation; grant Letters of Marque and Reprisal; coin Money; emit Bills of Credit; make any Thing but gold and silver Coin a Tender in Payment of Debts; pass any Bill of Attainder, ex post facto Law, or Law impairing the Obligation of Contracts, or grant any Title of Nobility.

No State shall, without the Consent of the Congress, lay any Imposts or Duties on Imports or Exports, except what may be absolutely necessary for executing it's inspection Laws: and the net Produce of all

Duties and Imposts, laid by any State on Imports or Exports, shall be for the Use of the Treasury of the United States; and all such Laws shall be subject to the Revision and Controul of the Congress.

No State shall, without the Consent of Congress, lay any Duty of Tonnage, keep Troops, or Ships of War in time of Peace, enter into any Agreement or Compact with another State, or with a foreign Power, or engage in War, unless actually invaded, or in such imminent Danger as will not admit of delay.

Article. II.

Section. 1.

The executive Power shall be vested in a President of the United States of America. He shall hold his Office during the Term of four Years, and, together with the Vice President, chosen for the same Term, be elected, as follows

Each State shall appoint, in such Manner as the Legislature thereof may direct, a Number of Electors, equal to the whole Number of Senators and Representatives to which the State may be entitled in the Congress: but no Senator or Representative, or Person holding an Office of Trust or Profit under the United States, shall be appointed an Elector.

The Electors shall meet in their respective States, and vote by Ballot for two Persons, of whom one at least shall not be an Inhabitant of the same State with themselves. And they shall make a List of all the Persons voted for, and of the Number of Votes for each; which List they shall sign and certify, and transmit sealed to the Seat of the Government of the United States, directed to the President of the Senate. The President of the Senate shall, in the Presence of the Senate and House of Representatives, open all the Certificates, and the Votes shall then be counted. The Person having the greatest Number of Votes shall be the President, if such Number be a Majority of the whole Number of Electors appointed; and if there be more than one who have such Majority, and have an equal Number of Votes, then the

House of Representatives shall immediately chuse by Ballot one of them for President; and if no Person have a Majority, then from the five highest on the List the said House shall in like Manner chuse the President. But in chusing the President, the Votes shall be taken by States, the Representation from each State having one Vote; A quorum for this Purpose shall consist of a Member or Members from two thirds of the States, and a Majority of all the States shall be necessary to a Choice. In every Case, after the Choice of the President, the Person having the greatest Number of Votes of the Electors shall be the Vice President. But if there should remain two or more who have equal Votes, the Senate shall chuse from them by Ballot the Vice President.

The Congress may determine the Time of chusing the Electors, and the Day on which they shall give their Votes; which Day shall be the same throughout the United States.

No Person except a natural born Citizen, or a Citizen of the United States, at the time of the Adoption of this Constitution, shall be eligible to the Office of President; neither shall any Person be eligible to that Office who shall not have attained to the Age of thirty five Years, and been fourteen Years a Resident within the United States.

In Case of the Removal of the President from Office, or of his Death, Resignation, or Inability to discharge the Powers and Duties of the said Office, the Same shall devolve on the Vice President, and the Congress may by Law provide for the Case of Removal, Death, Resignation or Inability, both of the President and Vice President, declaring what Officer shall then act as President, and such Officer shall act accordingly, until the Disability be removed, or a President shall be elected.

The President shall, at stated Times, receive for his Services, a Compensation, which shall neither be encreased nor diminished during the Period for which he shall have been elected, and he shall not receive within that Period any other Emolument from the United States, or any of them.

Before he enter on the Execution of his Office, he shall take the following Oath or Affirmation:—"I do solemnly swear (or affirm) that I will faithfully execute the Office of President of the United States, and will to the best of my Ability, preserve, protect and defend the Constitution of the United States."

Section. 2.

The President shall be Commander in Chief of the Army and Navy of the United States, and of the Militia of the several States, when called into the actual Service of the United States; he may require the Opinion, in writing, of the principal Officer in each of the executive Departments, upon any Subject relating to the Duties of their respective Offices, and he shall have Power to grant Reprieves and Pardons for Offences against the United States, except in Cases of Impeachment.

He shall have Power, by and with the Advice and Consent of the Senate, to make Treaties, provided two thirds of the Senators present concur; and he shall nominate, and by and with the Advice and Consent of the Senate, shall appoint Ambassadors, other public Ministers and Consuls, Judges of the supreme Court, and all other Officers of the United States, whose Appointments are not herein otherwise provided for, and which shall be established by Law: but the Congress may by Law vest the Appointment of such inferior Officers, as they think proper, in the President alone, in the Courts of Law, or in the Heads of Departments.

The President shall have Power to fill up all Vacancies that may happen during the Recess of the Senate, by granting Commissions which shall expire at the End of their next Session.

Section. 3.

He shall from time to time give to the Congress Information of the State of the Union, and recommend to their Consideration such Measures as he shall judge necessary and expedient; he may, on extraordinary Occasions, convene both Houses, or either of them, and in Case of Disagreement between them, with Respect to the Time of Adjournment, he may adjourn them to such Time as he shall think proper; he shall receive Ambassadors and other public Ministers; he shall take Care that the Laws be faithfully executed, and shall Commission all the Officers of the United States.

Section. 4.

The President, Vice President and all civil Officers of the United States, shall be removed from Office on Impeachment for, and Conviction of, Treason, Bribery, or other high Crimes and Misdemeanors.

Article III.

Section. 1.

The judicial Power of the United States, shall be vested in one supreme Court, and in such inferior Courts as the Congress may from time to time ordain and establish. The Judges, both of the supreme and inferior Courts, shall hold their Offices during good Behaviour, and shall, at stated Times, receive for their Services, a Compensation, which shall not be diminished during their Continuance in Office.

Section. 2.

The judicial Power shall extend to all Cases, in Law and Equity, arising under this Constitution, the Laws of the United States, and Treaties made, or which shall be made, under their Authority;—to all Cases affecting Ambassadors, other public Ministers and Consuls;—to all Cases of admiralty and maritime Jurisdiction;—to Controversies to which the United States shall be a Party;—to Controversies between two or more States;— between a State and Citizens of another State,—between Citizens of different States,—between Citizens of the same State claiming Lands under Grants of different States, and between a State, or the Citizens thereof, and foreign States, Citizens or Subjects.

In all Cases affecting Ambassadors, other public Ministers and Consuls, and those in which a State shall be Party, the supreme Court shall have original Jurisdiction. In all the other Cases before mentioned, the supreme Court shall have appellate Jurisdiction, both as to Law and Fact, with such Exceptions, and under such Regulations as the Congress shall make.

The Trial of all Crimes, except in Cases of Impeachment, shall be by Jury; and such Trial shall be held in the State where the said Crimes shall have been committed; but when not committed within any State, the Trial shall be at such Place or Places as the Congress may by Law have directed.

Section. 3.

Treason against the United States, shall consist only in levying War against them, or in adhering to their Enemies, giving them Aid and Comfort. No Person shall be convicted of Treason unless on the Testimony of two Witnesses to the same overt Act, or on Confession in open Court.

The Congress shall have Power to declare the Punishment of Treason, but no Attainder of Treason shall work Corruption of Blood, or Forfeiture except during the Life of the Person attainted.

Article. IV.

Section. 1.

Full Faith and Credit shall be given in each State to the public Acts, Records, and judicial Proceedings of every other State. And the Congress may by general Laws prescribe the Manner in which such Acts, Records and Proceedings shall be proved, and the Effect thereof.

Section. 2.

The Citizens of each State shall be entitled to all Privileges and Immunities of Citizens in the several States.

A Person charged in any State with Treason, Felony, or other Crime, who shall flee from Justice, and be found in another State, shall on Demand of the executive Authority of the State from which he fled, be delivered up, to be removed to the State having Jurisdiction of the Crime.

No Person held to Service or Labour in one State, under the Laws thereof, escaping into another, shall, in Consequence of any Law or Regulation therein, be discharged from such Service or Labour, but shall be delivered up on Claim of the Party to whom such Service or Labour may be due.

Section. 3.

New States may be admitted by the Congress into this Union; but no new State shall be formed or erected within the Jurisdiction of any other State; nor any State be formed by the Junction of two or more States, or Parts of States, without the Consent of the Legislatures of the States concerned as well as of the Congress.

The Congress shall have Power to dispose of and make all needful Rules and Regulations respecting the Territory or other Property belonging to the United States; and nothing in this Constitution shall be so construed as to Prejudice any Claims of the United States, or of any particular State.

Section. 4.

The United States shall guarantee to every State in this Union a Republican Form of Government, and shall protect each of them against Invasion; and on Application of the Legislature, or of the Executive (when the Legislature cannot be convened), against domestic Violence.

Article. V.

The Congress, whenever two thirds of both Houses shall deem it necessary, shall propose Amendments to this Constitution, or, on the Application of the Legislatures of two thirds of the several States, shall call a Convention for proposing Amendments, which, in either Case, shall be valid to all Intents and Purposes, as Part of this Constitution, when ratified by the Legislatures of three fourths of the several States, or by Conventions in three fourths thereof, as the one or the other Mode of Ratification may be proposed by the Congress; Provided that no Amendment which may be made prior to the Year One thousand eight hundred and eight shall in any Manner affect the first and fourth Clauses in the Ninth Section of the first Article; and that no State, without its Consent, shall be deprived of its equal Suffrage in the Senate.

Article. VI.

All Debts contracted and Engagements entered into, before the Adoption of this Constitution, shall be as valid against the United States under this Constitution, as under the Confederation.

This Constitution, and the Laws of the United States which shall be made in Pursuance thereof; and all Treaties made, or which shall be made, under the Authority of the United States, shall be the supreme Law of the Land; and the Judges in every State shall be bound thereby, any Thing in the Constitution or Laws of any State to the Contrary notwithstanding.

The Senators and Representatives before mentioned, and the Members of the several State Legislatures, and all executive and judicial Officers, both of the United States and of the several States, shall be bound by Oath or Affirmation, to support this Constitution; but no religious Test shall ever be required as a Qualification to any Office or public Trust under the United States.

Article. VII.

The Ratification of the Conventions of nine States, shall be sufficient for the Establishment of this Constitution between the States so ratifying the Same.

The Word, "the," being interlined between the seventh and eighth Lines of the first Page, The Word "Thirty" being partly written on an Erazure in the fifteenth Line of the first Page, The Words "is tried" being interlined between the thirty second and thirty third Lines of the first Page and the Word "the" being interlined between the forty third and forty fourth Lines of the second Page.

Attest William Jackson Secretary

done in Convention by the Unanimous Consent of the States present the Seventeenth Day of September in the Year of our Lord one thousand seven hundred and Eighty seven and of the Independance of the United States of America the Twelfth In witness whereof We have hereunto subscribed our Names,

G°. Washington

President *and deputy from Virginia*

Appendix III.

Bill of Rights

Amendment I

Congress shall make no law respecting an establishment of religion, or prohibiting the free exercise thereof; or abridging the freedom of speech, or of the press; or the right of the people peaceably to assemble, and to petition the Government for a redress of grievances.

Amendment II

A well-regulated Militia, being necessary to the security of a free State, the right of the people to keep and bear Arms, shall not be infringed.

Amendment III

No Soldier shall, in time of peace be quartered in any house, without the consent of the Owner, nor in time of war, but in a manner to be prescribed by law.

Amendment IV

The right of the people to be secure in their persons, houses, papers, and effects, against unreasonable searches and seizures, shall not be violated, and no Warrants shall issue, but upon probable cause, supported by Oath or affirmation, and particularly describing the place to be searched, and the persons or things to be seized.

Amendment V

No person shall be held to answer for a capital, or otherwise infamous crime, unless on a presentment or indictment of a Grand Jury, except in cases arising in the land or naval forces, or in the Militia, when in actual service in time of War or public danger; nor shall any person be subject for the same offence to be twice put in jeopardy of life or limb; nor shall be compelled in any criminal case to be a witness against himself, nor be deprived of life, liberty, or property, without due process of law; nor shall private property be taken for public use, without just compensation.

Amendment VI

In all criminal prosecutions, the accused shall enjoy the right to a speedy and public trial, by an impartial jury of the State and district wherein the crime shall have been committed, which district shall have been previously ascertained by law, and to be informed of the nature and cause of the accusation; to be confronted with the witnesses against him; to have compulsory process for obtaining witnesses in his favor, and to have the Assistance of Counsel for his defence.

Amendment VII

In Suits at common law, where the value in controversy shall exceed twenty dollars, the right of trial by jury shall be preserved, and no fact tried by a jury, shall be otherwise re-examined in any Court of the United States, than according to the rules of the common law.

Amendment VIII

Excessive bail shall not be required, nor excessive fines imposed, nor cruel and unusual punishments inflicted.

Amendment IX

The enumeration in the Constitution, of certain rights, shall not be construed to deny or disparage others retained by the people.

Amendment X

The powers not delegated to the United States by the Constitution, nor prohibited by it to the States, are reserved to the States respectively, or to the people.

End Notes

1st President George Washington

www.history.com/this-day-in-history-in-george-washington born/ www.history.com/this-day-in-history-george-washington died/

https://en.wkipedia.org http://www.rasmussen.edu/student-life/blogs/main/us-presidents-with-college-educations-from-learners-to-leaders/

http://www.ushistory.org/us

http://www.history.com

https://en.wikipedia.org/wiki/Shays%27_Rebellion

http://www.history.com

http://www.teachushistory.org/detocqueville-visit-united-states/articles/historical-background-traveling-early-19th-century http://www.teachushistory.org/detocqueville-visit-united-states/articles/roads-travel-new-england-1790-1840 http://eh.net/encyclopedia/turnpikes-and-toll-roads-in-nineteenth-century-america/

The 2nd President John Adams

www.google.com place of birth/place of death

http://www.let.rug.nl/usa/biographies/john-adams/education-and-early-career-(1745-1758).php
http://www.rasmussen.edu/student-life/blogs/main/us-presidents-with-college-educations-from-learners-to-leaders/

http://www.history.com/this-day-in-history/adams-passes-first-of-alien-and-sedition-acts;
http://www.history.com/topics/alien-and-sedition-acts

http://www.history.com/news/ask-history/what-was-the-xyz-affair; http://www.john-adams-heritage.com/the-xyz-affair/

The 3rd President Thomas Jefferson

www.google.com/placeofbirth/place

https://learnodo-newtonic.com/james-madison-accomplishments

http://faculty.montgomerycollege.edu/gyouth/FP_examples/student_examples/truc_huynh/education.html http://www.rasmussen.edu/student-life/blogs/main/us-presidents-with-college-educations-from-learners-to-leaders/

https://www.270towin.com/1800_Election/

http://.www.history.com lewis-clark

http://www.history.com topics/us-presidents

Www.google.com-ThomasJefferson-French Revolution

The 4th President James Madison

www.google.com/placeofbirth/place/deathplace

http://www.rasmussen.edu/student-life/blogs/main/us-presidents-with-college-educations-from-learners-to-leaders/

http://www.ohiohistorycentral.org/w/Battle_of_Lake_Erie / www.google.com Battle of the Thames

http://www.historyofwar.org/articles/battles_bladensburg.html www.google.com

https://www.britannica.com/event/Battle-of-Plattsburgh

https://.www.goggle.com francis scott-key.

https://learnodo-newtonic.com/james-madison-accomplishments

The 5th President James Monroe

www.google.com/placeofbirth/placeofdeath

http://www.millercenter.org. http://www.rasmussen.edu/student-life/blogs/main/us-presidents-with-college-educations-from-learners-to-leaders/

http://www.history.com/topics/monroe-doctrine: https://www.ourdocuments.gov/doc.php?flash=true&doc=23

The 6th President John Quincy Adams

www.google.com/placeofbirth/deathplace/

https://millercenter.org/president/jqadams/life-before-the-presidency

http://www.rasmussen.edu/student-life/blogs/main/us-presidents-with-college-educations-from-learners-to-leaders/

www.google.com

https://www.270towin.com/1824_Election/ http://www.history.com/this-day-in-history/presidential-election-goes-to-the-house http://www.ushistory.org/us/23d.asp

https://learnodo-newtonic.com/john-quincy-adams-accomplishments

http://www.history.com/topics/us-presidents/john-quincy-adams http://study.com/academy/lesson/john-quincy-adams-as-president-facts-accomplishments-quiz.html

The 7th President Andrew Jackson

www.google.com/placeofbirth/placeofdeath

https://www.thoughtco.com/andrew-jackson-7th-president-united-states-104317

http://www.rasmussen.edu/student-life/blogs/main/us-presidents-with-college-educations-from-learners-to-leaders/

https://www.270towin.com/1828_Election/ http://www.u-s-history.com/pages/h325.html https://en.wikipedia.org/wiki/United_States_presidential_election,_1828

https://www.loc.gov/rr/program/bib/elections/election1832.html

http://study.com/academy/lesson/election-of-1832-significance-history-quiz.html

http://www.presidency.ucsb.edu/showelection.php?_year=1832

http://www.history.com/this-day-in-history/andrew-jackson-narrowly-escapes-assassination;

http://www.history.com/news/andrew-jackson-dodges-an-assassination-attempt-180-years-ago

https://www.britannica.com/topic/nullification-crisis: http: www.u-s-history.com (Nullification Crisis)

http://www.u-s-history.com/pages/h333.html https://en.wikipedia.org/wiki/Nullification_Crisis

https://en.wikipedia.org/wiki/Worcester_v._Georgia

https://learnodo-newtonic.com/andrew-jackson-accomplishments

The 8th President Martin van Buren

 www.google.com/placeofbirth/placeofdeath

https://www.nps.gov/nr/twhp/wwwlps/lessons/39vanburen/39facts1.htm

https://millercenter.org/president/vanburen/life-before-the-presidency

http://www.rasmussen.edu/student-life/blogs/main/us-presidents-with-college-educations-from-

learners-to-leaders/

https://millercenter.org/president/martin-van-buren/key-events

www.history.com-Amistad

The 9th President William Henry Harrison

www.google.com/placeofbirth/placeofdeath

http://mentalfloss.com/article/69233/7-presidential-facts-about-william-henry-harrison

https://www.millercenter.org.president-harrison https://en.wikipedia.org/wiki/William_Henry_Harrison
 http://www.rasmussen.edu/student-life/blogs/main/us-presidents-with-college-educations-from-

learners-to-leaders/

The 10th President John Tyler

www.google.com/placeofbirth/placeofdeath

https://www.milercenter.org.

http://www.history.com/topics

 https://en.wikipedia.org/wiki/Whig_Party_(United_States)

https://www.biography.com/people/john-tyler-9512796

The 11th President James K. Polk

www.google.com/placeofbirth/placeofdeath

www.google.com http://www.miller.center.com-Polk http://www.rasmussen.edu/student-life/blogs/main/us-presidents-with-college-educations-from-learners-to-leaders/

https://www.thoughtco.com/the-mexican-american-war-2136186 https://www.shmoop.com/manifest-destiny-mexican-american-war/battles.html https://www.google.com https://ww.brittanica.com

http://www.history.com/topics/us-presidents/james-polk

The 12th President Zachary Taylor

www.google.com/placeofbirth/placeofdeath

https://www.thefamouspeople.com/profiles/zachary-taylor-154.php

https://www.biography.com/people/zachary-taylor-9503363 http://www.rasmussen.edu/student-life/blogs/main/us-presidents-with-college-educations-from-learners-to-leaders/

The 13th President Millard Fillmore

www.google.com/placeofbirth/placeofdeath

http://.www.miller.center.com-Fillmore http://www.rasmussen.edu/student-life/blogs/main/us-presidents-with-college-educations-from-learners-to-leaders/

The 14th President Franklin Pierce

www.google.com/placeofbirth/placeofdeath

http://enwikipedida.com http://www.rasmussen.edu/student-life/blogs/main/us-presidents-with-college-educations-from-learners-to-leaders/

www.google.com

https://www.ourdocuments.gov/doc.php?flash=true&doc=28 http://www.history.com/topics/kansas-nebraska-act http://www.ushistory.org/us/31a.asp

www.google.com

The 15th President James Buchanan

www.google.com/placeofbirth/placeofdeath

https://www.whitehouse.gov/1600/first-ladies/harrietlane:

http://www.firstladies.org/biographies/firstladies.aspx?biography=16

https://www.brainyquote.com/quotes/quotes/w/williamhs318361.html:

http://www.worldhistory.biz/modern-history/82286-william-h-seward-a-higher-law-than-the-constitution-march-11-1850.html

The 16th President Abraham Lincoln

www.google.com/placeofbirth/placeofdeath

https://www.nps.gov/gett/learn/historyculture/civil-war-timeline.htm

http://www.historynet.com/civilwar-battles

http://www.businessinsider.com/number-of-us-soldiers-who-died-in-every-major-war-2014-5

www.google.com

www.google.com

The 17th President Andrew Johnson

www.google.com/placeofbirth/placeofdeath

http://www.historychannel.com-presidents

http://m.georgiaencyclopedia.org/articles/counties-cities-neighborhoods/georgias-historic-capitals

https://constitutioncenter.org/blog/the-man-whose-impeachment-vote-saved-andrew-johnson:

The 18th President Ulysses Grant

www.google.com/placeofbirth/placeofdeath

http://www.history.com/news/the-black-friday-gold-scandal-145-years-ago

http://www.history.com/news/the-creditmobil scandal

http:www.history.com/grantscandals

http://www.history.com/topics/us-presidents/ulysses-s-grant

The 19th President Rutherford Hayes

www.google.com/placeofbirth/placeofdeath

http://www.rasmussen.edu/student-life/blogs/main/us-presidents-with-college-educations-from-learners-to-leaders/

https://www.270towin.com/1876_Election/

http://www.AmericanHistory-josephconlinvolumeII

The 20th President James Garfield

www.google.com/placeofbirth/placeofdeath

https://www.270towin.com/1876_Election/

https://www.googlecom.-Guiteau

https://www.biography.com/people/charles-julius-guiteau-235814

The 21st President Chester Alan Arthur

www.google.com/placeofbirth/placeofdeath

http://www.rasmussen.edu/student-life/blogs/main/us-presidents-with-college-educations-from-learners-to-leaders/

https://millercenter.org/president/cleveland/life-before-the-presidency

http://www.rasmussen.edu/student-life/blogs/main/us-presidents-with-college-educations-from-learners-to-leaders/

https://learnodo-newtonic.com/grover-cleveland-accomplishments

(http://www.republicanpresidents.net/10-interesting-facts-about-chester-arthur)

http://www.historycentral.com

The 22nd President Grover Cleveland

www.google.com/placeofbirth/placeofdeath

https://www.270towin.com/1884_Election/

The 23rd President Benjamin Harrison

www.google.com/placeofbirth/placeofdeath

https://www.270towin.com/1888 Election/

http://study.com/academy/lesson/benjamin-harrison-facts-presidency-accomplishments.html

The 24th President Grover Cleveland

www.google.com/placeofbirth/placeofdeath

https://www.270towin.com/1892 election

http://milercenter.org./cleveland before president http://www.rasmussen.edu/student-life/blogs/main/us-presidents-with-college-educations-from-learners-to-leaders/

The 25th President William McKinley

www.google.com/placeofbirth/placeofdeath

https://healthresearchfunding.org/3-major-accomplishments-of-william-mckinley/

www.google.com

www.goggle.com

http://study.com/academy/lesson/the-presidential-election-of-1896.html

 http://study.com/academy/lesson/the-presidential-election-of-1896.html

https://www.historyonthenet.com/authentichistory/1865-1897/4-1896election/index.html

https://www.historyonthenet.com/authentichistory/1865-1897/4-1896election/index.html

http:www.googlecom.-MicKinley

The 26th President Theodore Roosevelt

www.google.com/placeofbirth/placeofdeath

http://www.rasmussen.edu/student-life/blogs/main/us-presidents-with-college-educations-from-learners-to-leaders/

https://learnodo-newtonic.com/theodore-roosevelt-accomplishments

https://guycounseling.com/theodore-roosevelt-accomplishments/

https://infograph.venngage.com/p/175656/10-accomplishments-of-teddy-roosevelt

https://www.newsmax.com/FastFeatures/theodore-roosevelt-accomplishments-domestic/2014/08/26/id/591051/

http://www.historycentral.com/Bio/presidents/t_roosevelt.html

The 27th President William Howard Taft

www.google.com/placeofbirth/placeofdeath

https://millercenter.org/president/taft/domestic-affairs

https:enwikipedia.com./William Howard Taft

https://www.biography.com/people/william-howard-taft-9501184

www.google.com-William Howard Taft

The 28th President Woodrow Wilson

www.google.com/placeofbirth/placeofdeath

https://www.270towin.com/1912_Election/   https://www.britannica.com/event/United-States-presidential-election-of-1912 http://www.woodrowwilsonhouse.org/1912-election

https://www.270towin.com/1916_Election/   https://www.britannica.com/event/United-States-presidential-election-of-1916 http://www.woodrowwilsonhouse.org/1916-election

https://constitutioncenter.org/interactive-constitution/amendments/amendment-xvii

http://www.history.com/topics/18th-and-21st-amendments

https://www.ourdocuments.gov/doc.php?flash=false&doc=63

https://learnodo-newtonic.com/woodrow-wilson-accomplishments

https://learnodo-newtonic.com/woodrow-wilson-accomplishments

http://www.history.com/this-day-in-history/pancho-villa-attacks-columbus-new-mexico

https:www.google.com https://www.archives.gov/education/lessons/zimmermann

www.google.com-Lusitania-Sussex

https://quizlet.com/73053538/chapter-23-flash-cards/

https://www.googlecom./treaty of Brest-Litvosk

https://en.wikipedia.org/wiki/Spring_Offensive http://www.worldwar1.com/heritage/chthierry.htm

http://www.businessinsider.com/number-of-us-soldiers-who-died-in-every-major-war-2014-5

https://encyclopedia.1914-1918-online.net/article/war_losses_usa

https://en.wikipedia.org/wiki/Hundred_Days_Offensive

http://www.worldwar1luton.com/event/hundred-days-offensive

https://www.google.com

https://www.google.com

The 29th President Warren Harding

www.google.com/placeofbirth/placeofdeath

http://www.rasmussen.edu/student-life/blogs/main/us-presidents-with-college-educations-from-learners-to-leaders/

http://www.history.com/topics/teapot-dome-scandal

http://time.com/4000619/my-obsession-with-warren-hardings-mistress/ https://www.google.com

http://www.rasmussen.edu/student-life/blogs/main/us-presidents-with-college-educations-from-learners-to-leaders/

The 30th President Calvin Coolidge

www.google.com/placeofbirth/placeofdeath

https://healthresearchfunding.org/4-major-accomplishments-of-calvin-coolidge/

https://coolidgefoundation.org/presidency/coolidge-administration-accomplishments/

http://www.google.com.-Coolidge

The 31st President Herbert Hoover

www.google.com/placeofbirth/placeofdeath

http://www.google.com-Hoover

http://www.google.com/depression

https://www.historyonthenet.com/authentichistory/1930-1939/1-hoover/2-bonusarmy /

https://www.historyonthenet.com/authentichistory/1930-1939/1-hoover/2-bonusarmy /

The 32ⁿᵈ President Franklin Delano Roosevelt

www.google.com/placeofbirth/placeofdeath

http://www.zerohedge.com/news/what-30-years-gold-confiscation-us-government-looks (This is the congressional law that President Ford would actually sign Pub.L. 93-373,).

http://uscode.house.gov/statutes/pl/93/374.pdf https://www.huffingtonpost.com/steve-mariotti/when-owning-gold-was-ille_b_10708196.html /http://www.history.com/this-day-in-history/fdr-takes-united-states-off-gold-standard http://mentalfloss.com/article/12715/why-did-us-abandon-gold-standard

http://www.history.com/topics/world-war-ii/bombing-of-hiroshima-and-nagasaki

https://en.wikipedia.org However, by the time the atomic bombs are dropped F.D.R. is dead (he dies on April 12, 1945) and his successor Harry Truman orders the atomic bombs dropped on Japan on the dates mentioned above. Counting KIA, WIA, MIA, the U.S. suffered 1,076,245

http://www.businessinsider.com/number-of-us-soldiers-who-died-in-every-major-war-2014-5

https://www.secondworldwarhistory.com/world-war-2-statistics.asp

https://www.nationalww2museum.org/students-teachers/student-resources/research-starters/research-starters-worldwide-deaths-world-war https://en.wikipedia.org/wiki/World_War_II_casualties

www.google.com/search

www.google.com

The 33ʳᵈ President Harry Truman

www.google.com/placeofbirth/placeofdeath

http://www.rasmussen.edu/student-life/blogs/main/us-presidents-with-college-educations-from-learners-to-leaders/

https://www.270towin.com/1948_Election/ https://en.wikipedia.org/wiki/Executive_Order_9981 /

https://www.ourdocuments.gov/doc.php?flash=false&doc=84

http://www.google.com-Truman Doctrine

http://www.history.com/topics/cold-war/berlin-blockade

http://www.google.com

https://www.historyguy.com/korean_war_timeline.htm#.Whla02de7tQ

https://en.wikipedia.org/wiki/United_Nations_Security_Council_Resolution_82

https://www.historyguy.com/korean_war_timeline.htm#.Whla02de7tQ

https://www.deseretnews.com/article/865616489/This-week-in-history-China-enters-the-Korean-War.html

http://www.history.com/this-day-in-history/truman-relieves-macarthur-of-duties-in-korea

http://www.history.com/topics/douglas-macarthur http://www.cbs.news/Koreanwardead

https://www.historyguy.com/korean_war_casualties_and_statistics.htm

The 34th President Dwight D. Eisenhower

www.google.com/placeofbirth/placeofdeath

https://www.nps.gov/features/eise/jrranger/5accompx.htm

https://www.quora.com/How-did-Eisenhower-feel-about-Brown-v-Board-of-Education-He-took-measures-to-enforce-it-but-I%E2%80%99m-under-the-impression-that-he-did-so-reluctantly-Is-there-any-basis-for-this-thought

https://www.nps.gov/features/eise/jrranger/5accompx.htm

The 35th President John F. Kennedy

www.google.com/placeofbirth/placeofdeath

http://www.rasmussen.edu/student-life/blogs/main/us-presidents-with-college-educations-from-learners-to-leaders/

 http://www.history.com/this-day-in-history/the-bay-of-pigs-invasion-begins

https://www.quora.com/Who-said-success-has-many-fathers-but-failure-is-an-orphan

https://www.cia.gov/news-information/featured-story-archive/2016-featured-story-archive/the-bay-of-pigs-invasion.html

https://www.history.com/cuban missile crisis http://www.history.com/this-day-in-history/cuban-missile-crisis

https://www.nasa.gov/mission_pages/apollo/apollo11.html

The 36th President Lyndon B. Johnson

www.google.com/placeofbirth/placeofdeath

 http://www.rasmussen.edu/student-life/blogs/main/us-presidents-with-college-educations-from-learners-to-leaders/

http://www.americaslibrary.gov/jb/modern/jb_modern_polltax_1.html

https://www.our.documents.govt

https://www.our.documents.govt

https://www.raabcollection.com/lyndon-b-johnson-autograph/lyndon-b-johnson-promotes-his-great-society-programs http://www.dictionary.com/browse/great-society

https://www.colorado.edu/AmStudies/lewis/1025/greatgreatsociety.pdf

http://www.history.com/this-day-in-history/major-battle-erupts-in-the-ia-drang-valley

https://en.wikipedia.org/wiki/Battle_of_Ia_Drang https://www.thedailybeast.com/how-the-battle-of-the-ia-drang-valley-changed-the-course-of-the-vietnam-war

http://www.history.com/this-day-in-history/heavy-battle-rages-during-operation-junction-city

http://www.history.com/this-day-in-history/operation-junction-city-begins

http://www.dtic.mil/dtic/tr/fulltext/u2/a139612.pdf

https://en.wikipedia.org/wiki/Operation_Junction_City

http://www.google.com/Tet

http://www.historychannel.com/Tet

http://www.history.com/this-day-history/heavy-battle-rages-during-Tet

https:en.wikipedia.org/wiki/Tet-Offensive

https://en.wikipedia.org/wiki/sirhansirhan

The 37th President Richard Nixon

www.google.com/placeofbirth/placeofdeath

https://en.wikipedia.org/wiki/Peace_with_Honor

http://www.presidency.ucsb.edu/ws/?pid=4337 / https://www.nixonfoundation.org/2015/11/the-nixon-comprehensive-health-insurance-plan/

(http://www.vietnamgear.com/war1971.) 24,000 U.S. troops in at the end of 1972 left in Vietnam.(https://en.wikipedia.org/wiki/1972_in_the_Vietnam_War)

(https://www.thoughtco.com/vietnam-war-operation-linebacker) (https://www.thoughtco.com/vietnam-war-the-easter-offensive) http://www.historynet.com/north-vietnamese-armys-1972 http://www.pbs.org/kenburns/the-vietnam-war/episodes/

 https://www.google.com (https://www.thoughtco.com/vietnam-war-operation-linebacker II) https://en.wikipedia.org/wiki/Peace_with_Honor

(https://en.wikipedia.org/wiki/G._Gordon_Liddy)

the 38th President Gerald Ford

www.google.com/placeofbirth/placeofdeath

https://en.wikipedia.org/wiki/Twenty-sixth_Amendment_to_the_United_States_Constitution

http://www.history.com/topics/the-26th-amendment

https://www.fordlibrarymuseum.gov/library/document/factbook/vetoes.htm

https://www.senate.gov/reference/Legislation/Vetoes/vetoCounts.htm

http://www.sfgate.com/news/article/Ford-escaped-2-assassination-attempts- 2481771.php

http://www.history.com/this-day-in-history/gerald-ford-survives-first-assassination-attempt

https://en.wikipedia.org/wiki/Gerald_Ford_assassination_attempt_in_Sacramento

The 39th President Jimmy Carter

www.google.com/placeofbirth/

http://en.wikipedia.org.com http://www.rasmussen.edu/student-life/blogs/main/us-presidents-with-college-educations-from-learners-to-leaders/

https://www.google.com/search?q=When+was+the+Camp+David+accord+signed+between+Israel+and+Egypt%3F&rlz=1C1VSNG_enUS692US692&oq=When+was+the+Camp+David+accord+signed+between+Israel+and+Egypt%3F&aqs=chrome..69i57.17360j0j7&sourceid=chrome&ie=UTF-8

https://www.google.com

https://www.google.com http://www.rasmussen.edu/student-life/blogs/main/us-presidents-with-college-educations-from-learners-to-leaders/

The 40th President Ronald Reagan

www.google.com/placeofbirth/placeofdeath

https://www.270towin.com/1980_Election/

https://en.wikipedia.org/wiki/List_of_United_States_presidential_elections_by_Electoral_College_margin http://www.presidency.ucsb.edu/showelection.php?year=1980

https://www.270towin.com/1984_Election/ Reagan acquired 55, 455,000 popular votes to Mondale's 37,577,000 popular votes. Again, Reagan's presidential win was one of the largest both in electoral votes and popular votes. http://www.presidency.ucsb.edu/showelection.php?year=1984

https://en.wikipedia.org/wiki/List_of_United_States_presidential_elections_by_Electoral_College_margin

http://www.google.com/-Reaganairtrafficcontrollers

https://www.google.com/search?q=When+did+REagan+fire+all+the+air+traffic+controllers%3F&rlz=1C1VSNG_enUS692US692&oq=When+did+REagan+fire+all+the+air+traffic+controllers%3F&aqs=chrome..69i57j0l2.12852j0j7&sourceid=chrome&ie=UTF-8

http://www.topinspired.com/accomplishments-of-ronald-reagan/

http://www.presidency.ucsb.edu/reagan_100.php

http://www.history.com/this-day-in-history/reagan-refers-to-u-s-s-r-as-evil-empire-again

http://www.topinspired.com/accomplishments-of-ronald-reagan/

http://www.presidency.ucsb.edu/reagan_100.php

The 41st President George Herbert Walker Bush

www.google.com/placeofbirth/

http://www.rasmussen.edu/student-life/blogs/main/us-presidents-with-college-educations-from-learners-to-leaders/

http://www.history.com/news/the-strange-case-of-the-27th-amendment

https://constitutioncenter.org/interactive-constitution/amendments/amendment-xxvii

https://kids.laws.com/27th-amendment

breaking-new-taxes-pledge/gTMnk2hGmIbx4dlPsx8zTM/story.html

http://content.time.com/time/specials/packages/article/0,28804,1859513_1859526_1859516,00.html

https://www.govtrack.us/congress/bills/101/hr5835/summary / https://www.wikipedia.com

http://www.history.com/this-day-in-history/soviet-hard-liners-launch-coup-against-gorbachev

https://en.wikipedia.org/wiki/1991_Soviet_coup_d%27%C3%A9tat_attempt

Www.wikipedia.com / www.history.com First Persian Gulf War

https://en.wikipedia.org/wiki/Battle_of_the_Bulge http://www.historynet.com/battle-of-the-bulge

The 42nd President Bill Clinton

www.google.com/placeofbirth/

https://sfs.georgetown.edu/prominent-alumni/ https://www.snopes.com/bill-clinton-expelled-from-oxford/ https://en.wikipedia.org/wiki/Bill_Clinton#Law_school https://www.google.com

https://www.270towin.com/1992_Election/ https://www.britannica.com/event/United-States-presidential-election-of-1992

https://www.270towin.com/1996_Election/ / https://www.britannica.com/event/United-States-presidential-election-of-1996

https://en.wikipedia.org/wiki/Economic_policy_of_the_Bill_Clinton_administration

https://millercenter.org/president/bill-clinton/key-events

https://en.wikipedia.org/wiki/Economic_policy_of_the_Bill_Clinton_administration

https://www.theGuardian.com

http://www.factcheck.org/2008/01/clinton-passed-on-killing-bin-laden/

https://millercenter.org/president/bill-clinton/key-events

https://millercenter.org/president/bill-clinton/key-events

https://milercenter.org/president/bill-clinton/keyevents

www.wikedia.com

http://www.history.com/this-day-in-history/president-clinton-acquitted

https://millercenter.org/president/bill-clinton/key-events

The 43rd President George W. Bush

www.google.com/placeofbirth/

https://www.270towin.com/2000_Election/ Www.google.com

https://www.270towin.com/2004_Election/

http://www.telegraph.co.uk/news/worldnews/northamerica/usa/4242376/George-W-Bushs-10-Best-Moments.html https://www.google.com

http://www.weeklystandard.com/bushs-achievements/article/17066#

http://www.weeklystandard.com/bushs-achievements/article/17066#! http://www.history.com/this-day-in-history/president-bush-announces-military-action-in-afghanistan

http://www.telegraph.co.uk/news/worldnews/northamerica/usa/4242376/George-W-Bushs-10-Best-Moments.html

http://www.thirdworldtraveler.com/Politicians/Bush_accomplishments.html

The 44th President Barack Obama

www.google.com/placeofbirth/

(http://www.history.com/topics/us-presidents/barack-obama)

(https://en.wikipedia.org/wiki/Family_of_Barack_Obama)

The 45th President Donald Trump

www.google.com/placeofbirth/

https:// www.biography.com/people.-Trump

Conclusion

https://infogram.com/land-square-mileage-of-13-colonies-louisiana-purchase-land-and-land-to-be-bought-in-the-future-by-the-us-1gxop470jk31pwy

https://www.google.com/searchr&oq=What+is+the+total+square+miles+of+&aqs=chrome.0.0j69i57j0l4.20737j1j7&sourceid=chrome&ie=UTF-8

Appendix I

www.Declaration of Independence

Appendix II

The Founders' Constitution

Volume 1, Chapter 1, Document 8

http://press-pubs.uchicago.edu/founders/documents/v1ch1s8.html

The University of Chicago Press

www.google.com

Appendix III.

www.BillofRights.org

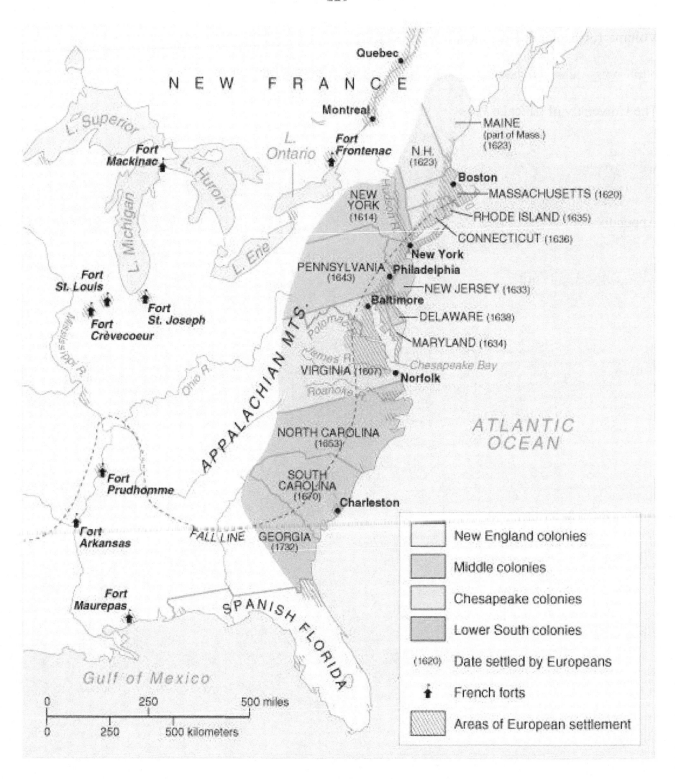

220

http://mrkash.com/activities/colonies.html

Source*https://www.google.com/search?q=A+Map+of+the+Continental+United+States

Made in the USA
Las Vegas, NV
25 September 2023